Thomas Wolfe's Characters

Thomas Wolfe's Characters

PORTRAITS FROM LIFE

by Floyd C. Watkins

NORMAN : UNIVERSITY OF OKLAHOMA PRESS

Library of Congress Catalog Card Number: 57-7335

Composed and printed at Norman, Oklahoma, U.S.A.,
by the University of Oklahoma Press.
First edition.

To Richmond Croom Beatty

Preface

In August, 1953, I went to Asheville, North Carolina, for the first time. For years I had read Thomas Wolfe's books and had heard rumors about his quarrels with his home town, and I had come to learn what I could about the conflict. Vaguely, too, I wished to see how the books compared with what he had known, and perhaps I had an obscure hope of finding some of the sources of his art.

I arrived at night, and at a time when Asheville seemed little different from any mountain town that caters to tourists. The next morning I looked out the window of my small room high in the George W. Vanderbilt Hotel. Tom's mountains rimmed in life, as he had said. Asheville was like the bottom of a cup. After breakfast, I asked the way to the square. The Confederate monument that adorns courthouse squares in the South has its representative in the granite spire in the center of Pack Square, but this monument was a memorial to Zebulon Baird Vance, Civil War governor of North Carolina. My memory tumbled about aimlessly before recognition and the first clue came. Here were Bear and Zack Joyner, those uncouth mountaineers of *The Hills Beyond*.

It was that easy. One must first know his Wolfe, and if

he does the materials and sources of the novels are inescapable. They are in the names of the streets and the buildings; nearly all the bronze tablets erected by the historical societies reveal the materials used by Wolfe's imagination. The newspapers, the histories of North Carolina, the records of the fire departments and the courts, the vital statistics, the banks—any record of life in Asheville is related to Wolfe and what he wrote. And the people remember what he wrote about; most of the bitterness is gone, and they talk.

Since that August, I have turned now to his works, now to the source. And this book is a record of what I have found, a comparison of fact and fiction, a study of what he imagined. It is, of course, impossible to document many of the sources for such information as this; some subjects must be treated obscurely; some not at all—at least during this generation. One must wait for the years to heal the sores of old wounds. Probably I have made errors, but I have checked for accuracy at every possible point.

As long as Wolfe lived he was annoyed and disconcerted because the citizens of Asheville constantly talked of what he had written about them. A few scholars have vaguely and fastidiously ventured to examine briefly how he used a few facts; no one has laid the subject as open as the libel laws will allow. There are still restrictions, but what can be written must be, since evidence and facts are being lost and forgotten every day.

In many instances it is almost impossible to distinguish between facts, Wolfe's imagination, and the imagination of the modern Ashevillian. The spirit of the researcher subjects him to the tendency to assume that there is no fiction in Wolfe's works, yet he must keep in mind Wolfe's contention that people remember things that never happened. In Asheville, it is easy to recall the novels and to think that they are life. In confronting this problem, I have tried always to rely on newspapers, city directories, and the like, instead of gossip and memory.

The reconstruction of the background of Wolfe's writings has led me to seek help in many and sometimes unusual places. I am indebted to many libraries and agencies, especially to the Long Beach Public Library, Long Beach, California; the Los Angeles Public Library; the Academy of Motion Picture Arts and Sciences; the Museum of Modern Art, New York City; the Library of Congress; the North Carolina Department of Agriculture; and the University of North Carolina Library. The entire staff of the Emory University library have given generously of their time and assistance. Liberal research grants from Emory University and from the University Center in Georgia have made it possible for me to gather material in Asheville. My colleagues in the English department of Emory University, especially Professors John C. Stephens, Jr., Edwin T. Martin, and Ward Pafford, have listened patiently and long to my monologues on Wolfe, and they have counseled wisely. Professors Richmond C. Beatty, of Vanderbilt University; J. O. Eidson, of the University of Georgia; and Bell I. Wiley and Pierre R. Loiseaux, of Emory University, have helped me willingly and unselfishly. Professor Thomas Daniel Young, of Mississippi Southern College, has read the entire manuscript and given helpful suggestions.

I am grateful to Charles Scribner's Sons for permission to quote from *Look Homeward, Angel, Of Time and the River, From Death to Morning,* and *The Story of a Novel;* and to Harper and Brothers for permission to quote from *The Web and the Rock, You Can't Go Home Again,* and *The Hills Beyond.*

Floyd C. Watkins

April 1, 1957
Emory University, Georgia

Contents

Illustrations

Thomas Wolfe's Characters

I. The Fabric of the Far and Lost

When thomas wolfe came home to Asheville, North Carolina, for the last time in the summer of 1937, one of the tourists he met in the mountain resort town was his friend F. Scott Fitzgerald, that professional protagonist of the Lost Generation. Fitzgerald told Wolfe then that he was wasting his talent by using the sterile materials of the barren Southern mountains and the small town. Wolfe's refutation, according to the story, was that Fitzgerald's Lost Generation had dissipated their vitality and that real life was to be found in the characters and stories of such people as Wolfe's old Uncle John Westall, who lived far back in the mountains in Burnsville, North Carolina. This example was on Wolfe's mind because he had just heard his uncle tell the story that he was to use as the basis of that wonderful short story and description of a battle, "Chickamauga," printed in *The Hills Beyond.*[1]

Wolfe's deep respect for these old mountaineers and his love for Asheville and the South are ironic when contrasted with his exile from them. His association with young cynics like Fitzgerald and Sinclair Lewis should have led him either to cosmopolitan and sophisticated subjects like Fitzgerald's or to

1 This story was told to me by Mrs. Mabel Wheaton, sister of Thomas Wolfe.

an urbane satirical attitude toward the town in which he was born. And there was contempt. Yet somehow Wolfe in Brooklyn and in Europe recalled Asheville and the South with love, poetry, and nostalgia. They furnished the fiber for his loom, and it was this material that controlled his subject matter, his attitude, and his art. His Southern heritage seems to have explained in part his antipathy toward the Lost Generation: "If Hunt *wants* to belong to The Lost Generation. . . ," Wolfe wrote of Fitzgerald in *You Can't Go Home Again,* "that's *his* affair. But he can't have me. If I have been elected, it was against my knowledge and my will—and I resign."[2] "The House of the Far and Lost," an earlier account of the Lost Generation in *Of Time and the River,* describes a Southerner's view of "the pursuit of pleasure" as the one interest of the lives of three Englishmen, who seek pleasure with "the madness of desperation, the deliberate intent of men to cover up or seek oblivion at any cost of effort from some hideous emptiness of the soul."

After Wolfe left Asheville for Harvard in 1920, he became physically as alienated from the place of his nativity as any of the more sophisticated young artists of his age. But studying at Harvard, teaching at New York University, and traveling in Europe, he strangely kept his mind focused on his homeland. The plays written at Harvard are set in Asheville, and the first novel, *Look Homeward, Angel,* is so closely modeled after Wolfe's experiences as a youth that it offers vast opportunities for a study of the psychology of memory. George Webber, Wolfe's spokesman in his last two novels, tries "to set down the shape and feel" of a year of his childhood.[3] And from this

[2] Thomas Wolfe, *You Can't Go Home Again* (New York, Harper and Brothers, 1940), 715.

[3] Thomas Wolfe, *The Web and the Rock* (New York, Harper and Brothers, 1939), 454.

endeavor comes the idea of his first novel, which comes to be, as he has hoped, "the picture, not merely of his youth, but of the whole town from which he came, and all the people in it just as he had known them." *All the people,* not just a few of the most memorable. For a man of lesser memory, the task would have been impossible; but, in London or in New York, Wolfe was able to "evoke and bring back the odors, sounds, colors, shapes, and feel of things with concrete vividness."[4] In *The Web and the Rock,* George Webber can "see and remember to their remotest detail every place where he had lived, every country he had visited, every street he had ever walked upon, everyone he had ever known or spoken to, together with the things they said and did. . . ."[5]

Indeed, this attempt to recapture a lost year by way of a sort of total recall is critically an able summary of Wolfe's methods in recording his life and compressing it eventually into four novels and two volumes of short stories. These with the huge stacks of still unpublished manuscripts would amount to an attempt to use in fiction all the life of Thomas Wolfe, alias Eugene Gant and Monk Webber. Here is one essential problem of this study: the function of recall and of creation in Wolfe's accounts of his life in Asheville and the South.

The things he chose to evoke in that first novel were Southern. After a day of writing in his ledgers, he declared in *The Story of a Novel,* he would remember "that I was born in North Carolina and wonder why the hell I was now in London lying in the darkened bed, and thinking about words I had that day put down on paper."[6] The words were mostly descriptions of remembered things, altered and adapted by cre-

[4] Thomas Wolfe, *The Story of a Novel* (New York, Charles Scribner's Sons, 1936), 31.

[5] *The Web and the Rock,* 455.

[6] *The Story of a Novel,* 7.

ative and emotional urges. The confusion between the fact remembered and the fiction created increased with the years, and even Wolfe could not remember what he had known and what he had imagined. It is possible to charge that he created nothing, and possible to maintain, as he did, that almost nothing is entirely true to fact.

Many Ashevillians know something of what is fact and what fiction, but they too with passing time have forgotten some things and created or imagined others. Despite these problems, it may be possible to re-create the fabric of the years and to see how Wolfe used what he had known. He has left many clues. He was, first of all, both careful and careless with a name, and some of his fictional nomenclature is fascinating to behold. The descriptive and meaningful name is almost as prevalent in his works as in those of Ben Jonson and Charles Dickens, yet the meaning is often evident only to those who know the factual basis of his fiction.

It is by now common knowledge that Wolfe's family plays a significant part in all his novels. In *Look Homeward, Angel,* the members of his mother's family are introduced very early (page 13), and they are central characters. Westall in fact became *Pentland* in fiction. ("Penland" is a prominent name in western North Carolina.) Thomas Pentland, Henry, Will, Jim, Elmer, Eliza, Bacchus, Greeley, and Thaddeus—all these are namesakes of real persons who were his mother's kin. "Gant" is the name given in fiction to Wolfe's immediate family. Only four names are the same in life and in art: those of the father, W. O.; the mother, Julia Elizabeth ("Eliza" in the novels); and the names of the twins, who died young in fiction as well as in fact—Benjamin Harrison and Grover Cleveland. The names of the living children were all changed.

Identification of names is certainly not definition of the creative powers of a writer, but in the works of Wolfe such delving turns up facts with several significances. His artful naming of his characters was one of the traits that led to such a furious reception of *Look Homeward, Angel,* and his method of changing names is an indication of the amount of autobiography in his work.

Many places are given names entirely different in sound from the real names but very similar in meaning, and the comparisons are interesting etymologically. Raleigh, North Carolina, for example, retains the name of an Elizabethan courtier and becomes *Sydney,* just as Old Fort, a town near Asheville, is in Wolfe's works *Old Stockade.* Chapel Hill is *Pulpit Hill,* and Spruce Street, the address of Mrs. Wolfe's boardinghouse, the Old Kentucky Home, becomes *Spring Street,* the address of Eliza Gant's *Dixieland.* Government Street Wolfe calls *Federal Street. Altamont,* the name for Asheville, connotes altitude and mountains, but appropriate as the name is, it is imaginary only as a name for Asheville, because there is a small town called Altamont in western North Carolina.

The nationality of names and of the characters in the novels is in almost every instance unchanged: Jeannerett becomes *Jannadeau;* Sternberg, *Greenberg;* Guischard, *Deshaye;* Finkelstein, *Stein;* Lipinski, *Rosalsky.*

Because of their vast estates and mansion near Asheville, the Vanderbilts have played significant roles in the life of the town and in Wolfe's novels. When he wrote about them, he associated the name of their sire, old "Commodore" Vanderbilt, the railroad baron, with that of another robber baron of the post–Civil War period, Jay Gould. Vanderbilt thus became *Goulderbilt.*

The connotation of grain as well as the *t-o-n* is preserved in the change from Wheaton to *Barton*. When Clara Paul became *Laura James*, as Mrs. Wolfe notes in *The Marble Man's Wife*, a similar ending for the first name was retained, and the last name was changed to that of a different disciple of Christ.

In many names one syllable is changed while another remains the same: Woodfin Street, where Wolfe was born, becomes *Woodson Street* in the novels. Biltmore, the Vanderbilt estate, is called *Biltburn*; Redwood, *Redmond*; Brigman, *Tugman*. The *Tarkington* family in *Look Homeward, Angel* were really Perkinsons; Israel became, obviously and logically, *Isaacs*. The fictitious *Montgomery Avenue* is in reality Asheville's Montford Avenue.

Only the initials are changed in many names: Bus Woody is changed to *Gus Moody*; Patton Avenue, to *Hatton Avenue*; Jarrett, to *Garrett*. Wolfe enjoyed playing with names in changing Reuben Rawls to *Ralph Rolls*, in reversing Charles French Toms to get *Tom French*.

Sometimes only one name is changed while the other, although it may be extremely unusual, is retained. Changes of this sort are numerous: Pearl Shope to *Pearl Hines*; Charlie Mascari to *Pete Mascari*; Cassius or "Cash" Gudger to *Saul Gudger*; Rufus Woodcock to *Gilbert Woodcock*; Charles L. Sluder to *Fagg Sluder*; Julius Martin to *Julius Arthur*; James Barnard to *Dirk Barnard*; Louis Graves to *George Graves*; Daniel Hodges to *Malcolm Hodges*.

The saloonkeeper O'Donnel, Wolfe calls *Tim O'Donnel*, but later in the same book he is given a different last name, *Tim O'Doyle*. Another such inconsistency is the spelling of the name of the groceryman as *Bradley* and *Bradly*. Jeweller Arthur M. Field is once called *Shields* and again *Arthur N. Wright*.

Why Wolfe throughout his fiction used names so near to the real ones is a speculation that Asheville has often considered. That he was aware of how he followed life and how he changed it seems to be proved by his usual care in giving entirely fictitious names to those involved in great scandals. His methods of naming characters perhaps helped him avoid the extra labor of keeping hundreds of strange names straight in his head. Perhaps, on the other hand, he wished his home-town friends to know the sources of his art. Did he realize how the use of a real name or one similar to it would increase the pleasure—or the anger? His consistency indicates that surely he must have enjoyed skirting the abyss and making fiction as close to life as possible.

Even the tourist casually driving through Asheville for the first time is able to identify some of the people and places of the novels. Old residents are still able to point out a remarkable number of things that Wolfe wrote about. Careful examination of old city directories, newspapers, telephone books—reinforced by conversations with local citizens and the identifications given in articles and stories—results in nearly complete equation of fiction and fact.

There are many more than 300 characters and places mentioned by name or described in *Look Homeward, Angel,* and probably there is not an entirely fictitious person, place, or incident in the whole novel. I have been able to identify with some accuracy about 250 places and people; and in almost every instance where the problem is difficult, there is evidence that Wolfe had in mind a real character or a place. Those migrant boarders and tourists who came to the Old Kentucky Home, rocked on the porch for a spell, and then moved on are seldom identifiable. Wolfe remembered them, but the townspeople do not; and the minor exploits of boarders rarely are recorded by the papers. The Negroes also have been forgotten. Wolfe recalled the sordid and strange details of their segregated lives, but their names in most instances are now lost. Fiction is here probably based on fact that cannot be proved. Some of Eugene's friends at the University of North Carolina have been hard to equate with those of Wolfe, but here again the research is difficult and the practice well established. On the other hand, when the character is of a type that is well known in a small town, there is hardly ever any difficulty.

When identification cannot be established for a family, a check in the city directories still reveals that Wolfe almost invariably used surnames that were prevalent in contemporary Asheville, and usually the social, economic, and racial status is unchanged in the fiction. Although there is no Tom Flack in the directories, for example, there are several Negroes with that family name.

The methods the townspeople use to identify the characters of the novels are critical comments on Wolfe's mode of creation. The temptation of the researcher is to think that everyone in Asheville was an abnormality and a strange caricature of mankind. But people, events, and places are now seen out of focus, with the books serving as a device that works all the wonders of a combination prism-camera-telescope-microscope. Wolfe remembered well, but frequently his memory adhered to the physical abnormality, the occupation, the odd personal habit, the peculiar mannerism, or the whispered story. "Wolfe makes his characters stand out—even those who have minor roles," wrote a local journalist in the *Asheville Citizen.* "He has a knack of selecting those peculiarities in characteristics which are easily forgotten by others but which tend to bring out certain vital phases of the real person."[7] One of his uncles, for example, commented that he did not realize how often he pared his nails until his nephew described it so frequently in his book. Clarence Sumner, still a reporter for the *Citizen* and once a classmate of Wolfe at the University of North Carolina, states that "Wolfe never fictionalized except to combine, emotionalize, caricature." Thus, he created his characters, exploiting all the eccentricities of his family and of those others whom he knew well, using other townspeople for background and unimportant roles. The good-humored, deformed, and somewhat idiotic Willie Goff, the seller of pencils, is a good example. In fiction his name, personality, and deformities are described as truthfully by Wolfe as they are by the *Citizen's* reporter in a reminiscent article on local characters.[8]

Many times he seems to have exaggerated or satirized by making changes in fact. Although he gave many occupations correctly, he called one man an electrician when he is listed in the city directory as a consulting engineer. Is this satire on presumption? There is one confusion of names, perhaps unintentional, perhaps comic, that involves race and religious relations. In that famous account of Eugene's paper route, there occurs the following description of the Negro church:

From the worn central butte round which the colony swarmed, the panting voices of the Calvary Baptist Church mounted, in an exhausting and unceasing frenzy, from seven o'clock until two in the morning, in their wild jungle wail of sin and love and death. The dark was hived with flesh and mystery. Rich wells of laughter

[7] *Asheville Citizen,* March 23, 1932.

[8] Thomas Wolfe, *Look Homeward, Angel* (New York, Charles Scribner's Sons, 1929), 342; *Asheville Citizen,* August 22, 1948.

bubbled everywhere. The catforms slid. Everything was immanent. Everything was far. Nothing could be touched.[9]

There is, however, no Negro Calvary Baptist Church in Asheville, but in West Asheville there is a white Calvary Baptist Church, and there is a Negro Calvary Presbyterian Church. Did Wolfe forget the denomination and thus satirize accidentally, or was he, as a Presbyterian, bantering the Baptists?

But Wolfe forgot very little. As he said in *The Web and the Rock,* he was creating "the picture . . . of the whole town . . . and all the people in it. . . ." The details he remembered are remarkable. Grover, in *Look Homeward, Angel* as in life, lived twelve years and twenty days. The flood that prevents the honeymoon of Eugene's sister Helen and Hugh Barton is an accurate description of a flood that did delay in fact as in fiction the honeymoon of Wolfe's sister and her husband and was as devastating as Wolfe described it.

Satire similar to that on the Calvary churches, but much more obvious to the outsider, is given in the description of the Shakespearean pageant, which was presented in 1916 by the Asheville schools. Wolfe's humor is startlingly emphasized by a comparison of his account in *Look Homeward, Angel* with that in the newspapers. Wolfe and the paper described the same parts of the program and the same people with only a few exceptions. The reporter, perhaps with the same instincts and passions, also noted Rosalind, whom Wolfe describes as "a ripe little beauty from the convent."[10] The tone, however, is revealingly different. The newspaper account is the usual description of a pageant: "Never perhaps in the history of Asheville

[9] *Look Homeward, Angel,* 302–303.
[10] *Ibid.,* 374.

has so beautiful an out-of-door spectacle delighted the eyes and stirred the emotions of the onlookers as that of yesterday in the charming little natural amphitheater at Albemarle park."[11] Humor distinguishes Wolfe's writing from that in the paper. There are Dr. George B. Rockham, the pompous "Voice of History," in the dress of the Restoration period to display "the charms of muscular calves"; "the little Jews," passing by "with the nobly marching music of 'Onward, Christian Soldiers' "; and Eugene Gant, dressed as a clown after his costume that was to make him Prince Hal is torn to pieces in attempts to make it cover his huge frame. This passage reveals a comedy the newspaper reporter could not risk and probably did not see. It should also serve as one answer to those critics who think Wolfe an egomaniac who always took himself too seriously in the character of Eugene Gant.

Satire is again the dominant motif when Wolfe presents William Jennings Bryan as one of the characters in a series of poetic and satiric vignettes. Here again a comparison of journalism and fiction reveals Wolfe's genius. While everyone was awaiting Bryan's appointment as secretary of state, he arrived in Asheville on December 18, 1912, for a speaking engagement and much backslapping. His address was on "The Making of a Man." (Wolfe apparently did not remember this title; it is hard to imagine him foregoing such an opportunity for satire.) Like the preacher who was "agin sin," Bryan was for the Sermon on the Mount, a moral order, and Christianity. After the speech, he remarked, according to the *Asheville Citizen*, "that he shall carry away memories of Asheville so delightful that he will not be satisfied until he visits here again with his

[11] *Asheville Times.*

family."[12] In the same vein as the newspaper, Wolfe's Commoner tells a minister, "Our only regret . . . is that our visit here must be measured by days and not by months. Nay, by years."[13]

But Bryan was apparently a paradox to Wolfe, for he is both praised and ridiculed. There is, on the one hand, Wolfe's poetry. As Bryan was questioned by a reporter, "The years of his glory washed back to him upon the rolling tides of rhetoric —the great lost days of the first crusade when the money barons trembled beneath the shadow of the Cross of Gold, and Bryan! Bryan! Bryan! Bryan! burned through the land like a comet." On the other hand, when asked about his retirement, "the Commoner answered characteristically with the following beautiful quotation from Longfellow." But the quotation Wolfe gives is somewhat inaccurately taken from Tennyson's "Locksley Hall":

> *When the war-drum throbbed no longer,*
> *And the battle-flags were furled*
> *In the Parliament of man,*
> *The Federation of the world.*

Apparently this is a deliberate error. Wolfe is having fun with Bryan's or the reporter's knowledge of poetry, and the reader is expected to perceive.

The uncanny memory of the entire Wolfe family is demonstrated best of all, except for Wolfe's works, in the biography of his mother, *The Marble Man's Wife*. Here is found the confirmation of details about the family as they appear in *Look Homeward, Angel* and as they lived in Asheville. The ages,

[12] *Asheville Citizen*, December 19, 1912.
[13] *Look Homeward, Angel*, 339–41.

the deaths, the personalities of these people in fact and in fiction correspond. Mrs. Wolfe gives an account of Mr. Wolfe's three marriages, especially of the second to Cynthia, who was in life and in fiction much older than her husband. There are descriptions of Tom Wolfe's trip to Norfolk, told of Eugene in *Look Homeward, Angel*; of Bessie Wolfe, nurse of Ben Wolfe and Ben Gant; of Mr. Wolfe's fame as a lavish provider; of her own people; and of a tubercular's hemorrhage in the Old Kentucky Home. This book, in short, recalls the town as it was seen by Miss Eliza; and for those who cannot go to Asheville, it offers the best opportunity for literary detective work.

Sometimes the vast superiority of fiction to fact is quite evident. Eugene Gant's idyllic love for Laura James culminates in a romantic picnic trip across lordly hills and into a cove, "the wooded cup of the hills." But *The Marble Man's Wife* reveals that Tom Wolfe and Clara Paul were accompanied (and therefore chaperoned) by a small boy.

The exaggeration of traits of the real people Wolfe wrote about is typical of his use of the members of his own family. Everyone who has known and written about Mrs. Wolfe has commented on her sharp memory and her talkativeness. Helen Gant is a somewhat exaggerated description of Tom's sister Mabel. Similarly, the weaknesses of Little Stevie are taken from the characteristics of Frank Wolfe; and W. O. Gant's wild torrent of rhetoric, his passions, his cleanliness, his love of food, roaring fires, and drink are taken from Wolfe's father. Here in real life was a man who, because of his son's great talent, became one of the most human, dynamic, and lovable characters in all fiction. That his character was essentially recorded, perhaps not always with exaggeration, may be seen from the memories of those who knew him and from his surviving letters, parts of which sometimes sound exactly as if they had been lifted from the speeches of W. O. Gant.

After the death of Ben in *Look Homeward, Angel,* surely modeled after one of the most tragic events in Tom Wolfe's life, there is a five-page description of a trip to the undertaker's by Luke (Fred Wolfe) and Eugene.[14] This incident offers an excellent opportunity for the comparison of fact and fiction in Asheville and Altamont. Wolfe's own factual version is found in a letter written to his former teacher, Mrs. Margaret Roberts, probably in 1923, six years before the publication of the *Angel.* Between this factual description and the fiction there are few real differences. The omission in the letter of the long passage about Horse Hines's sales talk on the coffin indicates that Wolfe either recorded more in the book or that he created this scene imaginatively. In the letter Wolfe described very generally the exhibition of the body by the undertaker: "He was proud of his job. It was one of the best he had ever done. No other undertaker could do a better one. Then, with true artistic pride, he began to point out the little excellencies in his finished work that showed the hand of the master."[15] But in the creative account he included many more specific details, specific actions, good dialogue, and better characterization:

"There!" he said, with deep satisfaction; and, rouge-stick in hand, head critically cocked, like a painter before his canvas, he stepped back into the terrible staring prison of their horror.

"There are artists, boys, in every profession," Horse Hines con-

[14] *Ibid.,* 567–72.

[15] Thomas Wolfe, "Writing Is My Life," *Atlantic Monthly,* Vol. CLXXVIII, No. 6 (December, 1946), 61–62.

tinued in a moment, with quiet pride, "and though I do say it myself, Luke, I'm proud of my work on this job. Look at him!" he exclaimed with sudden energy, and a bit of color in his gray face. "Did you ever see anything more natural in your life?"[16]

There is, furthermore, in the fiction an excellent description of the emotion of grief and the reactions to the viewing of the body:

Nothing of Ben could be buried here. In this poor stuffed crow, with its pathetic barbering, and its neat buttons, nothing of the owner had been left. All that was there was the tailoring of Horse Hines, who now stood by, watchfully, hungry for their praise.

Finally, the factual account of the laughter is a simple statement: "I went into howls of uncontrollable laughter." This sentence becomes in the novel a one-half-page description, somewhat macabre, of Eugene's howls of laughter at the undertaker's art. The literalness of Wolfe's use of the incident, despite the expansion, may be illustrated by the fact that in both accounts Eugene-Tom laughs, but Luke-Fred does not.

Wolfe's life at the University of North Carolina is as exactly followed as that in Asheville is. The university's *Carolina Magazine* has described the death of his sophomore roommate, Edmund Burrick, whom Wolfe calls Bob Sterling in *Look Homeward, Angel.*[17] The campus activities, editing, writing, and debating, that Eugene participates in so furiously were the activities of young Tom Wolfe. The description of the instructor's accusing Gant of using a "jack" in the translation of his Latin despite his having worked it out himself is based closely

[16] *Look Homeward, Angel,* 570–72.

[17] *Ibid.*, 480–82; Agatha Boyd Adams, *Thomas Wolfe: Carolina Student* (Chapel Hill, University of North Carolina Library, 1950), 32.

on reality. The portraits of his instructors in his book are largely based on campus "characters," whom people who have attended the university can still remember.

Except for the principle of exaggeration, there seem to be few discoverable conscious and consistent methods involved in the transposition of fact to fiction. To illustrate the ways of fusing and blending events and characters, the angel itself is one of the most interesting and complex examples. It helps to portray W. O. Gant's character; it has an emotional and symbolic significance for Eugene Gant and perhaps even more for Tom Wolfe. No great thematic or plot significance, however, can be attributed to it. Indeed, the one incident of the narrative in which it figures prominently is comic and relatively minor. The story recounts W. O. Gant's selling the angel to a much-admired proprietor of a house of ill fame. Her "figure was trim and strong," and she "had a great deal of energy, distinction, and elegance in her manner." She comes to buy a memorial for one of her poor girls, recently departed, and she selects the angel that Gant curses loudly in public but loves in secret: "It had come from Carrara in Italy, and it held a stone lily delicately in one hand. The other hand was lifted in benediction, it was poised clumsily upon the ball of one phthisic foot, and its stupid white face wore a smile of soft stone idiocy."[18]

Angels sold by Mr. Wolfe are standing in cemeteries all over western North Carolina, and for twenty years such publications as *Life* and the local papers carried stories about Wolfe and selected various angels to illustrate them. Not until 1949 was the real angel discovered in a cemetery in Hendersonville, North Carolina. The description in the novel follows most of the details of this angel. Other angels that have been used as

[18] *Look Homeward, Angel,* 267.

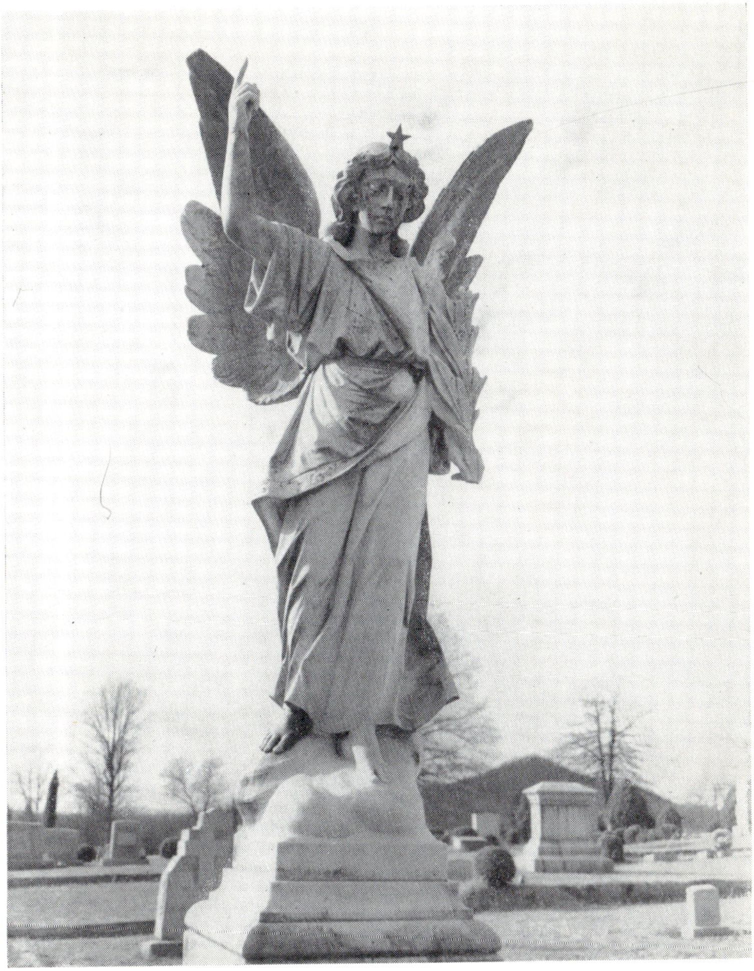

Courtesy Barber, Hendersonville, N. C.

W. O. Wolfe's "Angel." *"It had come from Carrara in Italy, and it held a stone lily delicately in one hand. The other hand was lifted in benediction, it was poised clumsily upon the ball of one phthisic foot, and its stupid white face wore a smile of soft stone idiocy."*

illustrations for articles fit in a few respects, but none of them holds "a stone lily delicately in one hand," and none of them is "poised clumsily upon the ball of one phthisic foot." There are two minor variations that Wolfe used to fit the story into the narrative. Most of that "smile of soft stone idiocy" appears in fiction rather than on the puzzling face of the real angel. Perhaps Wolfe had forgotten the real expression of the lips; perhaps he made her smile ironically because she was standing over the grave of a prostitute. The hand is lifted, but not in benediction. The real angel looks at the grave while spiritually pointing heavenward and apparently urging the dead to arise. The fictitious gesture of benediction is also ironic because the blessing is extended to a prostitute. Whether Wolfe forgot or changed can never be determined.

Here, it seems to me, is a significant commentary on Wolfe's creative genius. He is never vague, abstract; he never loosely describes several objects; he may mix details from different things and he may alter, but never is there a general blur without specific detail. It might be added not only that Wolfe used his excellent memory but also that he could not have written so well without it. And of course this method will not serve for other writers. How can one living in England remember the way a marble angel held a lily and the way the angel stood when it was last seen over twenty years before, when one was only five years old and living in the mountains of the South?

Although Wolfe was mainly a poetic recorder in his description of the statue, there is much fiction in the narrative about its being sold. W. O. Gant, the maker and seller of tombstones, is a fairly literal reproduction of Wolfe's father, and the woman who buys it in fiction was well known locally in fact. In reality she did not, however, buy the angel Wolfe described. He may simply have remembered her and the angel and have imaginatively created the scene that describes its purchase. Actually, the angel was sold for the grave of the wife of a gentleman who was president of a college in Mississippi, and it is probable that Wolfe did not know whose grave it marked. Here the satire and humor that could be explosively dangerous was accidental and unintentional.

The angel also provided opportunity for satiric and comic writing about the sentimentality of the tombstone salesman and his epitaphs. The purchaser decides on an inscription of two sentimental quatrains. A long, careful search and many inquiries about a possible source for this poem have produced no results. Probably Wolfe himself wrote the poem. It is doubly comic and satiric because it is the epitaph of a prostitute. Every single line can be read in terms of a sentimental bewailing of the departed, but almost every line can also refer ironically to the life of a prostitute:

> *She went away in beauty's flower,*
> *Before her youth was spent;*
> *Ere life and love had lived their hour*
> *God called her, and she went.*
>
> *Yet whispers Faith upon the wind:*
> *No grief to her was given.*
> *She left* your *love and went to find*
> *A greater one in heaven.*

Wolfe's artistic improvement of fact is emphasized by the comparison of this poem with the true, simple, and sincere inscription on the angel described: "Her children arise up, and call her blessed." Here fiction, then, is much more effective than life.

Even more than in the episode dealing with the angel, Mr.

Gant's character was the focus of interest when Wolfe quoted a letter that he wrote to his daughter Helen while she was on a singing tour. His sentiment, vitality, and gusto are revealed in his reactions to local events, especially the tragedy of the killing of John Duke.[19] And all his writing deals with people of Asheville and incidents that really happened in the town. When the Wolfe family letters are published or made available to researchers, it is possible that this letter will be found to have a source in a real letter written to some member of the family. A much greater likelihood, however, is that the letter as written in the novel conveys the tone of Mr. Wolfe's conversations and letters in general. "God knows," Mr. Gant writes rhetorically to his daughter, "what we'll all come to before the end of this fearful, hellish, and damnable winter, but I predict the poorhouse and soupkitchens like we had in the Cleveland administration." He has passed the windows of the Southern Fuel Company (really the Southern Coal Company) and seen the owner "with a fiendish smile of gloatation on his face as he looked out on the sufferings of the widows and orphans." Then follows his account of his son Eugene. Even Preston Carr, "who's sure to be the next governor" (really Locke Craig, governor of North Carolina from 1913 to 1917), has suggested that Gene be sent to the state university law school. Mr. Gant mentions a suit he has bought for his son at Moale's (there was a store owned by a man named Moale in Asheville).

The very human elements of Gant's character appear most vividly in the tale he tells about the death of John Duke. His love for women is shown in his attitude toward Duke's wife: "My heart bled for her. She's a pretty little woman." Duke was killed because of his drunken belligerence, and the suffering of

19 *Ibid.*, 317.

his wife evokes the heavy-drinking Gant's prohibitionist sympathies: "Liquor has caused more misery than all the other evils in the world put together." In this incident the hodgepodge of fact and fiction is again intriguing. The event on which Wolfe based the death of John Duke was the killing of a local scoundrel by the house detective of the Langren Hotel, which Wolfe calls the Whitstone, when Wolfe was twenty years old and far away studying at Harvard University.[20] But the letter in *Look Homeward, Angel* is written in the winter of Eugene's fourteenth year, 1915—six years before the main event described. Mrs. Mabel Wheaton, a singer like Helen Gant, gave up her career in 1915, and thus she could not have received from her father a letter containing this news while she was on a singing tour. In this passage Wolfe has closely followed fact while altering it to develop character and changing its time to suit his own purposes.

Here also is an instance where fiction is not so violent as fact. Mr. Gant records merely that the character Duke was "drunk and threatening to shoot everyone" and that he was "a terror when he drank." The prototype of this character, according to the *Asheville Citizen,* was even more ferocious. He had been "a fugitive from justice," he had been involved in numerous "episodes in courts," he had been tried for bootlegging and perjury, he had run for sheriff and amassed a grand total of seventy-eight votes, and he had owned a "road house" that in one raid by the law yielded a "freight car load of liquors and wines." Dramatic as these incidents are in the history of a desperado of Buncombe County, Wolfe never used them. Possibly he did not know them, perhaps because the letter from his family or the story as it was told to him was incomplete;

20 *Asheville Citizen.*

certainly the luridness of the actual facts would have detracted from Gant's comic moralizing on liquor.

Another method was Wolfe's using for pathos an incident that had been comic to him in his youth. He describes how Eugene Gant and Max Israel are "shaken by sudden glee" as they watch an orthodox Jew wailing about the suicide of his son, who has drunk carbolic acid.[21] He makes no comment on their glee, no condemnation of it. The facts of the actual suicide, also by carbolic acid, are recorded in the county's vital statistics. Possibly the reactions of the boys are just as literally described.

Seldom is there evidence in the early novels of Wolfe's having worked directly from any source other than his near-perfect powers of recall, either of the things he saw or of those he heard his family tell about. In one instance, however, there seems to be reliable evidence that he looked directly at a photograph as he wrote. In the description of the wedding of Helen Gant to Hugh Barton, he describes the bride and groom as "limply astare—frightened," the brothers of the bride as "widely, sheepishly agrin; Eliza, high-sorrowful and sad; Mrs. Selborne [really Mrs. Osborne] and a smile of subtle mystery; the pert flower-girls; Pearl Hines' [Pearl Shope] happy laughter."[22] These terms are so peculiarly apt and well chosen for the facial expressions of the persons in the picture of Mr. and Mrs. Wheaton's wedding that the inevitable conclusion is either that Wolfe deliberately used a photograph to prod his memory or that he could remember for over ten years a fleeting and momentary facial expression.

Other incidents seemingly based on fact prove, after re-

21 *Look Homeward, Angel,* 97.
22 *Ibid.*, 385.

search, to have some basis in life but to be mostly fiction, perhaps because Wolfe had never exactly known the true incidents he wished to recall. That marvelous series of vignettes on Altamont waking, in the fourteenth chapter of the *Angel*, includes a description of the sleeping girls at the Convent School of Saint Catherine's on Saint Clement's Road, really St. Genevieve-of-the-Pines, established in 1908 on Starnes Avenue, very near the "Old Kentucky Home." Either Sister Theresa is a figment of the imagination or she was Mother Deplanck. And the book by Sister Theresa, "modestly intended for school children, which has since celebrated her name wherever the noble architecture of prose is valued—the great *Biology*," apparently never existed. What Wolfe had in mind, if anything, is not now discoverable. The Mother Superior in 1953 had been teaching there twenty-five years and had attended the school before that, but she remembered no book written by one of the nuns in the history of the school. This may be one of the most purely fictitious passages in *Look Homeward, Angel*. The dormitory, with its "long cool glade of roseleaf sleeping girls,"[23] must have been inaccessible except in Wolfe's imagination.

Possibly some of these methods of using Asheville may be explained by what Wolfe was taught at the University of North Carolina. He was a student of Frederick Koch and a member of the Carolina Playmakers, one of the most prominent little theater groups in the decade after World War I. It was their primary assumption that a young playwright must write about what he knows and that if he is to succeed artistically he must be concerned with the culture and tradition in which he was bred. This theory accounts not only for the success of the Playmaker group but also perhaps for the artistic methods of

[23] *Ibid.*, 186.

their most famous member, Thomas Wolfe. Already in those early plays written at the university, Wolfe was using native scenes and basing the action upon plots taken directly from life. "In my one act play, the Return of Buck Gavin," Wolfe writes in a manuscript in the Koch Collection of the university, "the incident of the story was derived from a newspaper clipping describing the capture of a Texas outlaw in a Chicago tenement house." And this theory went with Wolfe to Harvard. A young Ashevillian who saw a production there of Wolfe's *Welcome to Our City* was horrified to find herself able to identify precisely every character in the play.[24]

That this exactness of Wolfe's use of memory continued even after he forsook the dramatic form for the narrative is shown in the statement of Edward C. Aswell, now the executor of the estate and over the years perhaps Wolfe's most steadfast defender: "I doubt if there was a character in it [*Look Homeward, Angel*] who was not drawn from someone he had known."[25] Maxwell Perkins, Wolfe's first editor, wrote to James Jones describing "the horror with which I realized, when working with Thomas Wolfe on his manuscript of 'The Angel,' that all these people were almost completely real, that the book was literally autobiographical."[26] And when Perkins discovered later that Wolfe was using just as literally some of the people at Scribner's as characters in his later novels, he thought of offering his resignation, although he believed that

24 Richard S. Kennedy, "Wolfe's Harvard Years," in Richard Walser (ed.), *The Enigma of Thomas Wolfe* (Cambridge, Harvard University Press, 1953), 30–31, and based on Richard S. Kennedy's "Thomas Wolfe at Harvard, 1920–1923," *Harvard Library Bulletin*, Vol. IV (Spring and Autumn, 1950).

25 Edward C. Aswell, "Introduction" to *You Can't Go Home Again* (New York, Harper's Modern Classics, 1941), ix.

26 Maxwell E. Perkins, *Editor to Author*, edited by John Hall Wheelock (New York, Charles Scribner's Sons, 1950), 296.

Wolfe had "the same right to make use of them as of anyone else in the same way. . . ."[27]

There is incontrovertible evidence that Wolfe knew that his first novel was autobiographical and that even before publication he was apprehensive about its reception. Several times he cautioned his mother to say nothing about the book before it came out. He wrote his favorite teacher, Mrs. Margaret Roberts and the prototype of Mrs. Margaret Leonard in the novel, that he feared "this book will wound and anger people deeply—particularly those at home."[28] Here he may have been thinking especially of Mrs. Roberts and trying to prepare and warn her, but she became one of those most deeply hurt by the novel. Some years before *Look Homeward, Angel* was published, Wolfe told J. M. Roberts, Jr., "If I write this book, and I must write it, for I must write, and it is all I have to work with, they'll never let me stand here again."[29]

These statements introduce an ambiguity of attitude, self-contradiction, and inconsistency. Despite his fears expressed to Mrs. Roberts and her son, Wolfe directly contradicted himself ten years later in *The Story of a Novel*, one of the most revealing accounts of methods of composition ever published by an American author:

> I can honestly say that I did not foresee what was to happen. I was surprised not only by the kind of response my book had with the critics and the general public, I was most of all surprised with the response it had in my native town. . . . For months the town seethed with a fury of resentment which I had not believed possible.[30]

[27] *Ibid.*, 124.

[28] Wolfe, "Writing Is My Life," *Atlantic Monthly*, Vol. CLXXIX, No. 1 (January, 1947), 44.

[29] *Asheville Citizen*, January 26, 1947.

[30] *The Story of a Novel*, 17–18.

Perhaps Wolfe simply forgot. In view of his basic honesty and innocence, indeed naïveté, there can hardly be any other explanation.

On his last trip home before *Look Homeward, Angel* appeared, Wolfe insisted to his friend George W. McCoy that his book was "no man's portrait" and asked McCoy to help prevent misunderstanding and to explain to the townsmen that the novel "was not an almanac of personal gossip."[31] "I think," Wolfe said before any Ashevillian had read the work, "it is only fair that a book should be read in a writer's home town in the same spirit it is read outside." Had he truly and literally given no man's portrait, he would have had no need for such help and understanding. Ignoring setting and place, one of the great elemental strengths of the *Angel*, Wolfe had insisted to McCoy after publication that the book was "not written about people North, South, East, or West but about all the people who ever lived." And so it was. But its very universality, Wolfe forgot, is attributable to the truth of the local people whom he portrayed. In all the complicated relationship between the author and his people, he seldom was unaware of Asheville's attitude toward him. He declared to McCoy that he valued and hoped to keep the respect and friendship of his home town, that, indeed, a young man is eager for "the commendation of people he likes."[32]

The first page of Wolfe's first published book, written before the storm of controversy and all the complications, is a statement "To the Reader," perhaps the best single evaluation of his autobiographical methods. Here he admits writing "of experience [not from imagination] which is now far and lost, but which was once part of the fabric of his life." At the

[31] *Asheville Citizen*, September 18, 1938.
[32] *Ibid.*

time when he wrote this statement he had no answer for the charge of autobiography, but he expected understanding, he said, from "those persons whom the writer may have known in the period covered by these pages." Here too is a good definition of the art that he contributed. "Fiction," he said, "is fact selected and understood, fiction is fact arranged and charged with purpose." According to this statement, then, Wolfe saw his own creation as fact plus arrangement, purpose, and understanding—surely the primary functions of any creative talent. No writer can treat what he does not know; even fantasy is based on comparison with some sort of reality. Perhaps the question really is—how large are the blocks he uses? Where another author depends on sand and gravel, Wolfe carved enormous blocks from the quarry. The dimensions and the architecture of the work, however, may, in the long run, be the same.

Despite Wolfe's prepublication, confidential admissions of autobiography, and his consequent fears, he quite honestly did not have, I believe, a premonition of how drastic would be the results of his airing the town's scandals and secrets to the world. Once the book was an accomplished fact, his attitude changed, and the emotional and intellectual reactions became resentful, rebellious, and complicated almost beyond comparison and analysis. One of the things he did in later years was frequently to describe his very practices just for the purpose of denial and condemnation. "A writer must use what is his own," he told a reviewer for the *New York Herald Tribune* in 1935. "But that is not to say that my first book was intended to be a faithful picture of Asheville, North Carolina, or of any other place on earth I have ever known."[33] Completely forgotten or ig-

[33] Julian R. Meade, "Thomas Wolfe on the Use of Fact in Fiction," *New York Herald Tribune Books,* Vol. XI, No. 32 (April 14, 1935), 8.

nored by this time, especially when an article about him was involved, was that plan described in *The Web and the Rock,* to picture "the whole town from which he came, and all the people in it just as he had known them." All the people and places that once had been printed indelibly on his own brain and that were still well remembered by the townsmen of Asheville were not now easily recalled. Then Wolfe continued this interview by telling the reporter that a writer "does not write by calling Greenville Jonesville [he could not more clearly have denied his own practices if he had used Raleigh and *Sydney*—actually in his next book Greenville, South Carolina, was to be called *Blackstone,* South Carolina] or by changing the names of Brown and Smith to Black and White [this denial would not be more specific if he used Vanderbilt-*Goulderbilt* or Israel-*Isaacs*]."[34] Then Wolfe declared that if this method were possible anyone could record a town and be a writer. What he ignored here were all the other component parts of his genius, which usually did record and change Brown and Smith to Black and White.

These fears of autobiography and the denials that Wolfe issued for years after the storm are only one aspect of the very changeable mind of an imaginative author. In print and to his friends Wolfe made many admissions of his excessive use of fact. The story of his death published in the *Asheville Citizen* quoted his statement that often a young author "turns too directly to the raw material he has before him."[35] The best criticism that George Webber's *Home to Our Mountains* ever received, he said, was the town drunk's statement that a man

[34] *Ibid.;* Thomas Wolfe, "You Can't Escape Autobiography," edited by Robert D. Meade, *Atlantic Monthly,* Vol. CLXXXVI, No. 5 (November, 1950), 80.

[35] *Asheville Citizen,* September 16, 1938.

could write about a horse thief but that he was not compelled to give such details as telephone number and address;[36] and in the later books he had learned, he wrote Edward Aswell, not to take his characters "so much from specific recollection," as he had in his first book, but to compact them "from the whole amalgam and consonance of seeing, feeling, living and knowing many people. . . ."[37]

Wolfe's description in *You Can't Go Home Again* of the publication of the first novel of Monk Webber is again autobiographical. Webber has, says Wolfe, written about his home town "with a nakedness and directness which, up to that time, had been rare in American fiction."[38] *Rare,* probably not in artistic realism, but in truth: Theodore Dreiser, Sinclair Lewis, and James T. Farrell had been most devastatingly direct in their treatments of fictional people. The truth of this phrase seems to have stuck in Wolfe's mind, because exactly two hundred pages later in the same novel Webber again thinks about his having written with "naked directness and reality that was rather rare in books."[39]

The basic factors in Wolfe's writings and in any evaluation of them are his family, his community, and his university; and these elements are with him much more determining forces than they are with most writers. The history and customs of his subjects called for "naked directness" and realism, satire, and idol-breaking. Asheville and the many crosscurrents of life there to be observed are the very matrix of his art.

The mountains surrounding the town on all sides may have hemmed in life, as Wolfe said in *Look Homeward, Angel,* but

[36] Aswell, "Introduction" to *You Can't Go Home Again,* x, and text, 358.
[37] Aswell, "Introduction" to *You Can't Go Home Again,* xii.
[38] *You Can't Go Home Again,* 126.
[39] *Ibid.,* 326.

certainly they did not dam it out. The story of Asheville essentially is one of the influx of the world. The mountaineer girl now has her mail-order dress and a radio, perhaps even television, and the strains of popular songs like "I Love Paris" prove that an alien culture has been carried into the homes of those whom W. O. Gant calls "mountain grills." But the distant lure of the hills long ago established such precedents. The ancestors of these very mountaineers were drawn to the site of Asheville by the wonders of the Blue Ridge ranges as they could be seen from the Piedmont region of North Carolina. Wild and strong-blooded frontiersmen, who were the forerunners of the modern far and lost hillmen, dispersed the wilder Indians, but in western North Carolina there are more survivals of the older cultures than are to be found in other regions of America. The reservation of the Cherokee Indians is not far from Asheville, and the Indian woman with a papoose on her back and a small tribe of little Indians beside her is still to be seen occasionally in the streets of the town.

These elements of the far and lost mingle with some of the most cosmopolitan Americans, the sport-shirted, tired, surly tourists and the bright businessmen who minister to their needs. The influx began significantly with George Vanderbilt, that most famous of all the tourists who have gravitated to what Ashevillians like to call "The Land of the Sky." In most of his works Wolfe has described the vast estates and the castle of this son of one of the greatest of the American robber barons after the Civil War. For five years, between 1890 and 1895, Vanderbilt was constructing that magnificent, depressing, unhomelike, forbidding 125-room castle, set in the midst of a huge estate that in 1905 consisted of one hundred and forty thousand acres of land once owned by Anglo-Saxon mountaineers, who could never have dreamed of such opulence. Thus, Asheville now, as in Tom Wolfe's youth, can display the primitive and proverbial log cabin culturally juxtaposed with Vanderbilt's medieval castle and its imported collections of priceless European plunder. There are Italian marble lions of the sixteenth century, carvings of the knightly and aristocratic "Return from the Chase" and of scenes from Wagner's operas, gold and silk tapestries that depict the loves of Venus and Mars and that probably bedecked the tent of Francis I at the Field of the Cloth of Gold, the chess table in which Napoleon's heart rested as it was reportedly smuggled into France after his death, a library of twenty thousand ornately printed and lavishly bound volumes, and the furnishings of Cardinal Richelieu. "And in a curious way that great estate had shaped the whole life of the town," Wolfe himself observed in *Of Time and the River.* "At the heart of the town's desire was the life of that great house." What an empty heart and desire and house!

This is but one of the structures built in Asheville by the newcomer barons of America. There is also the tremendous Grove Park Inn, built by the developer of Dr. Groves's chill tonic. Asheville is today partly a conglomeration of tourist motels and partly a site of relics of a more glorious and exploited past. The Asheville-Biltmore College has been established in Overlook or "Seely's Castle," built by the daughter and son-in-law of E. W. Grove at a cost of several hundred thousand dollars. Modeled on the Forde Abbey, twenty-five miles from London, the building was left incomplete exactly as the abbey was so that the copying would be exact. It was constructed by Italian workmen after they had finished the Grove Park Inn.

One who tours this city, which is a relic of a bygone age of

American attempts to become aristocratic, feels somehow that the mountaineer culture in its very simplicity was superior and that somehow here is a symbol of the picture of Altamont and Asheville's tragic flaw. It is also, one must not forget, the raw material of Wolfe's works. The intercourse of Asheville with the tourists begot the boom and resulted in the prostitution of the mountains and the simplicity of the life they had fostered. And there is still the mark of illegitimacy on the children they have bred. Those boarders leisurely rocking on the front porch of Eliza Gant's Dixieland were tourists paying their currency for the hospitality of a prosperous descendant of the hill-bound. The very blood of Tom Wolfe was a mixture of the drifting Yankee lured by the wonders of the mountains and of one of the mountaineers from "over yonder in Zebulon," who sold books to the tourists and the newcomers, who married out of the tribe to the Yankee, who catered to tourist boarders, and who speculated in land that constantly rose in price because of the hopes of more tourist trade.

This is the material and the conflict, the source of the poetry, the memory, and the rhetoric. Cosmopolitan and provincial Asheville gave Wolfe his background, furnished the mores of his novels, and gave him his subjects and his characters. Perhaps Asheville and his mother provided him with his tradition and his constant provincialism, his desire to come home again. With its tales of far-off wonders, as described by the tourists, the town and the blood of his father gave him his wanderlust. There were reasons for his being torn, attracted, and repelled. It was his very nature and the nature of his town and of his family.

The character of the town also intruded into the Wolfe and Gant family. The bourgeois character of the invading tourists perhaps explains the excessive concern of some of them for social standing. "I don't believe in cheap things"—this is a standard they often reiterate. Helen Gant is shocked when she realizes that her dying father's best friends are the honest, common working men who cluster together away from the prominent citizens when they visit him during his last sickness in *Of Time and the River*. That Puritan strain in the mountaineer is an innate characteristic of the Pentlands, the Gants, and Aunt Maw of the Webber cycle. The primitiveness and the luxury of Asheville are both to be found in the Old Kentucky Home, now a shrine to Wolfe's memory. An old, intricately fashioned sterling silver coffee urn stands in the dining room, and from its table the modern tourist can see the primitive kitchen with several wrought-iron wood stoves. On the wall hangs a beautiful piece of china that Mr. Wolfe bought especially to hang his watch on at night, but it contrasts strangely with the cheap iron beds of the many bedrooms. Such incongruence might be illustrated over and over, for it was a basic characteristic of Tom Wolfe's surroundings. The Old Kentucky Home is so much like Dixieland that one who enters the house for the first time feels as if he were rereading the book. Wolfe has described minutely and accurately the rooms and the furniture of the old boardinghouse.

In the final analysis, *Look Homeward, Angel* is a portrait not only of the ego of Wolfe but also of a Southern town. The unbelievably large number of characters does indicate that he succeeded in portraying, as George Webber wishes to do, "the whole town from which he came, and all the people in it just as he had known them." This book was but a beginning, and all the other novels, even those after the change from the Gant

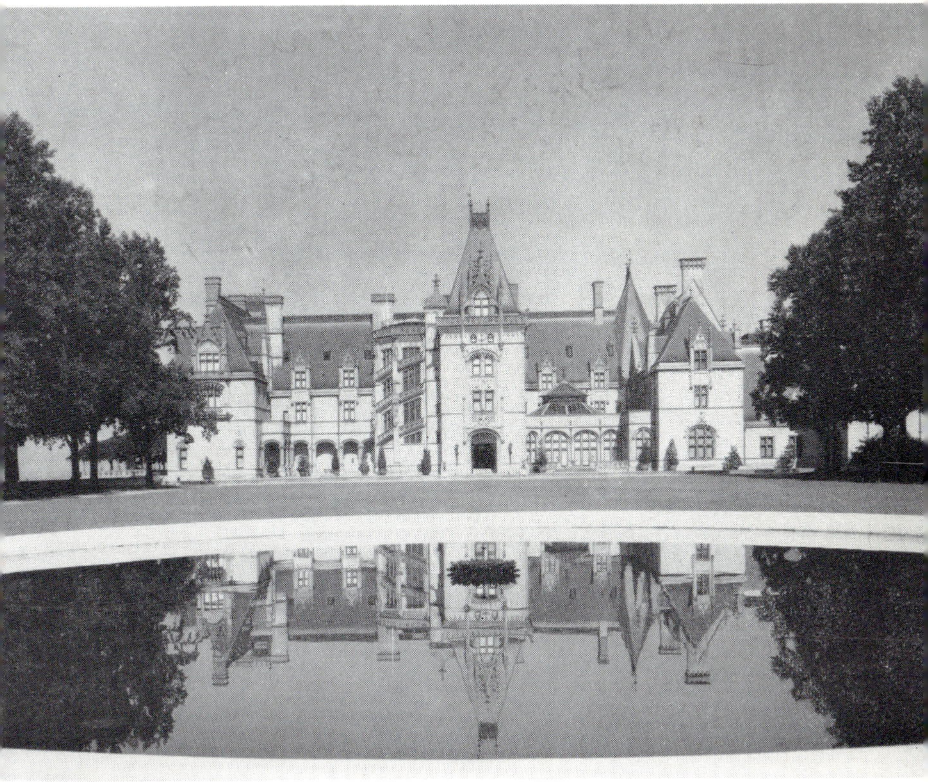

"Biltmore House," the Vanderbilt estate near Asheville, North Carolina.

to the Webber hero and family, continue to portra
town, the same places and people.

Altamont is a portrait of a town that is as fully pop
as Spoon River or Main Street or Winesburg, Ohio. Wolfe's writings are at times just as satiric, just as realistic, and just as bold as those of the most caustic Midwesterners, and this is what was to make the people of Asheville run mad with anger. There are, however, additional qualities in his writings that are not to be found in the books about the other imaginative towns. Masters, Lewis, and Anderson forgot the poetry and the innate goodness and mystery of man found in the simple folk of the local colorists; but Tom Wolfe, unlike most of his contemporaries, was able to conjoin realistic descriptions with some feeling, goodness with depravity. This achievement, perhaps, accounts for his great popularity among the American middle class, who have not yet turned naturalistic or esoteric.

Wolfe saw poetry and romance and nobility in the citizens of his town, and the almost unalleviated sterility of Lewis' Main Street is not to be found in Altamont. Despite the burliness and bawdiness of Doc McGuire, for example, there is a strain of great nobility in his rather depraved soul, as there is also in the honorable but dishonored aristocrats of Faulkner's Yoknapatawpha. No character with the vitality and gusto of McGuire and old Gant or with the brusqueness and love of Ben ever lived in Main Street.

Young Eugene Gant does hear the locomotive whistles calling him to wander, but Tom Wolfe the wanderer died while he had in progress a book on the Southern mountaineers. Their vitality served him as literary raw material all his life. Even his accounts of life in Brooklyn and at Harvard reveal a satire and a barrenness of incident and romance that are never to be found in the sections of his books about North Carolina and the South. No Altamontian ladles out his life in coffee spoons. One need not be a Confederate to deplore sometimes his failure to concentrate entirely on the land of his birth. It gave him the richest material he ever used, and *Look Homeward, Angel,* the only novel entirely with a Southern setting, remains his best book perhaps because comparatively he failed with alien people, settings, and materials.

Besides the appeal of exaggerated, comic, robust, tragic, and absurd characters, Wolfe permeated his works with a lyric strain that caused great admiration despite the lack of discipline. Often his poetry files off the edge of the satire and mysteriously contributes the feeling that regardless of satire, the portrait is essentially one of love. Two volumes of collected poetic passages from his works and the admiration of his readers testify to his lyricism, demonstrable from the poetic prose on the flyleaf of *Look Homeward, Angel* to the lyrical lament about the death of his brother Ben. Wolfe added much satire and lyricism by numerous quotations from the great poetry of all ages. Nearly every one of the forty-two pages in chapters XXIII and XXIV has several quotations lifted from great poems.[40] With a peculiar aptness and irony, Wolfe succeeded in making the borrowed verses comment on characters in Altamont. Negro laundresses at work, for example, are described in terms of one of Herrick's love lyrics: they plunge "their wet arms into the liquefactions of their clothes."

The books Wolfe read as a child and the motion pictures he saw also compose part of the background of the novel. Prob-

[40] Floyd C. Watkins, "Thomas Wolfe's High Sinfulness of Poetry," *Modern Fiction Studies.* Vol. II, No. 4 (December, 1956).

ably that cheap fiction which causes the dreamy young Eugene to think of himself as the heroic Bruce Eugene is taken literally and specifically from the pulp fiction of the time. The *Asheville Citizen* in 1914, for example, ran as a serial novel Harold MacGrath's *The Adventures of Kathlyn.* The hero, John Bruce, who saves Kathlyn in India, may have stayed in Wolfe's mind and served as the inspiration for the great Bruce that causes young Gant to call himself Bruce Eugene.

The description of the old silent wild western that Eugene has just seen with his father follows with the usual minutiae of detail many aspects of *The Fugitive,* a 1916 western starring the famous William S. Hart. Many of the actions and characters are almost identical in the motion picture and the novel, but apparently Wolfe also used vivid portions of other old westerns that he had seen as a child. The result of the combination is a paradoxical blending of satire on early movies and the wonders of romantic boyhood.

All these elements enter the lifelike portrait of youth spent in Asheville. And most of them point to a sympathy with the provincial, the rural, and the small town that was seldom to be encountered when *Look Homeward, Angel* appeared in 1929. It is no wonder that a cosmopolitan and urbane Fitzgerald thought Wolfe was wasting his time. Rather, the wonder is that Wolfe did not agree.

2. Save in His Own Country

THE SUDDEN APPEARANCE of the corpse of William Shakespeare on Asheville's Pack Square, left there by his resurrected townsmen from Stratford who had murdered him for portraying Stratfordians as clowns in the plays, would hardly have caused more excitement in Asheville than did the appearance of *Look Homeward, Angel* in the bookstores. Although there had been a few complimentary notices about the coming publication of a first novel by a local boy, no one was prepared for the events to come. Moldy skeletons had been taken from closets and hung on the tall monument in the middle of the square.

There had been novelists in the town before. Olive Tilford Dargan, poet, dramatist, and novelist, had been living in western North Carolina for years and in West Asheville since 1925. In 1920, James Hay had written a mystery novel, "*No Clue!*", and its reception in the newspapers had been such an ironic foreshadowing of the problems with Wolfe that the long-forgotten account demands comparison. A local columnist created a mountain character named "Colonel Blank Babers," who commented on the novel, and he was amazed at his first encounter with fiction. After discovering "to his vast surprise" that the events and people were imaginary, the Colonel declared his opposition to fiction: " 'I never knowd they was sech doin's a gwyne on,' said the Colonel to the crowd which gathered around him on the square. 'Folks a printin' books which they aint nary word er truth in 'em. I 'spects mebbe they order be a leggislater law agin sech like they aint a lot er laws which they orter be. . . .' "[1] And the Colonel's puzzlement raised the problem that has plagued Ashevillians and Wolfe's critics ever since: The Colonel was told by the bookseller that the characters in the novel "don't live nowheres. He says he jest made up all them things outen his head . . . they allers told me ef you see sunthin' in a book hit's bound fer to be so, an' now ef I reads a book I can't nowise tell ef hit's so er aint so." If the author of this jest had been responsible for Tom Wolfe's decision to write a book that was "so," he would have been the object of his neighbors' wrath in 1929.

What Wolfe thought the town expected of a novelist may be seen in his entirely fictitious account in *You Can't Go Home Again* of the story printed in the local newspaper about the forthcoming book by George Webber. Webber's statement to a reporter that the book is about a family in Old Catawba becomes the headline "LOCAL BOY WRITES ROMANCE OF THE OLD SOUTH." The inspired reporter expects Webber (and therefore Wolfe) to record "that stirring period of Old Catawba's past [which] has never before been accorded its rightful place of honor in the annals of Southern literature," and he inaccurately quotes Webber as hoping to "commemorate the life, history, and development of Western Catawba in a series of poetic legends comparable to those with which the poet Longfellow commemorated the life of the Acadians and the folklore of the New England countryside."[2] Despite

1 *Asheville Citizen*, February 14, 1921.
2 *You Can't Go Home Again*, 124.

such romantic delusions of grandeur, North Carolina's past was recorded, although not quite in the way expected by the fictitious reporter.

The jolting and shocking reviews of the novel in North Carolina newspapers presented an utter contrast to whatever glorious hopes the people had had for Wolfe's first novel. Ashevillians were not so deluded, unfortunately for Wolfe, as the critic for the *Boston Evening Transcript* who thought that the narrative was set in Pennsylvania! At least they knew beyond any doubt whatsoever the setting in time, place, and people. The *Asheville Citizen*, the more dignified and detached of the two local papers, tried to remain objective and to see the novel as an outsider would. "Life burns," the reviewer ironically and perhaps naïvely remarked, "with the deep colors of human emotions and richly marked characters."[3] The description of the use of fact in the novel was embedded in a critical account of "a genius' combination of reality, which will not shrink from even the most sordid details of everyday life, and of a child-like expression of the most delightful fantasy."

Walter S. Adams' review in the *Asheville Times* was more realistic and perhaps more willing to agitate. He commented that Wolfe had written the *Angel*, "sparing nothing and shielding nothing." If Wolfe had described the town, he had also described himself, and the reviewer eagerly attacked the self-portrait: "His life here, as he boldly sketches it, was crowded with pain, bitterness and ugliness." Because of the "frankness and detail rarely ever seen in print" and the reviewer's belief that "virtually all the characters are residents of this city," he predicted that the townsfolk would be "shocked into chills" and "severely annoyed," that some would "snicker and laugh"

[3] *Asheville Citizen*, October 20, 1929.

at this "autobiography of an Asheville boy." Although Adams admitted that "the outlander" might find "unquestioned literary merit," although he himself praised the "portraiture," "narrative," and "style," he ended his attack by charging that Wolfe had "dragged forth into the light . . . any scandal" that previously had "enjoyed only a subterranean circulation."[4] When Wolfe read this review, he called it "unfairly personal," although the review in the *Citizen* had been, he thought, "splendid."[5] Refuting the *Times,* he wrote his mother that every major character revealed "a heroic spirit" in a crisis, that the family should not "be greatly concerned with what spiteful and petty people in small towns think."[6]

Perhaps the most vituperative review was published in a paper outside Asheville. Writing in the Raleigh *News and Observer,* Jonathan Daniels used the headline to charge that Wolfe had turned his fury upon the South and his native state. Thomas Wolfe, he said, had "gone the way of rebels"; there was a "reign of terror of his talent." "In 'Look Homeward, Angel,' North Carolina, and the South are spat upon." Coming from a fellow student and college friend, that statement must have hurt the sensitive young novelist, who had convinced himself that he had drawn a portrait of love. Perhaps this is one of the statements Wolfe had in mind when he wrote in *You Can't Go Home Again,* "They leveled against him the most withering charge they could think of, and said he was 'not Southern.' "[7]

If there was any love in the book, Daniels did not see it:

[4] *Asheville Times,* October 27, 1929.
[5] *Thomas Wolfe's Letters to His Mother,* edited by John Skally Terry (New York, Charles Scribner's Sons, 1943), 188. (Hereafter referred to as *Letters to His Mother.*)
[6] *Ibid.,* 191.
[7] *You Can't Go Home Again,* 337.

"Against the Victorian morality and the Bourbon aristocracy of the South," he argued, "he has turned in all his fury and the result is not a book that will please the South in general and North Carolina in particular." The optimistic note of the review was the hope that Wolfe was getting "this little score paid off to his own country" and that he would be able to proceed to another work "in greater serenity of spirit." Even the lyricism was in Daniels' opinion very bad: "It is a book written in a poetic realism, the poetry of dissolution and decay, of life rotting from the womb, of death full of lush fecundity." Then he speculated on the cause of this expectoration and vengeance, settling on the family as the source of the bitterness: "Seeing any section through the Gant family," he believed, "would be like looking upon that section through the barred windows of a madhouse." The family too had been drawn in bitterness, and the result in the novel was "a life stirred only by the raw lusts for food and drink and sex and property." Of them all, he wrote, only Ben was "drawn with tenderness and feeling." As a foil to the madhouse of the lustful Gants, there was the lustful community, and here Daniels believed that a catalog of the characters would best serve his purposes, and he listed "prostitutes, white and black; loose women, Negroes and dope-fiends, drunken doctors, tuberculars, newsboys and teachers." The book was too strong a wine; Daniels found too much "blood and sex and cruelty." Finally, there was the charge of excessive use of fact in fiction. The account in the *Angel* of the University of North Carolina, as Daniels remembered the university, was "almost pure reporting."

Ashevillians did not need to be told by reviewers how to react to this book. They saw their sins as well as their virtues recorded in print, and on the first reaction all the poetry did not alleviate the luridness of the descriptions of their previously hidden errors. *Look Homeward, Angel* was so vividly true and factual that people recognized themselves and their neighbors; descriptions of the townspeople were so clear that a reader either discovered real sins he did not know about or believed as fact fictitious sins that his neighbor had not committed. The latter, of course, caused more bitterness. Discussions of the book intruded into almost every imaginable kind of gathering in the community, into club programs, garden club parties, card games, and bank directors' meetings. Wolfe's sister, Mrs. Mabel Wheaton, was shocked and deeply hurt because she was so obviously ignored when she attended one of her clubs. People bought copies because they had heard that they were described, sent copies to friends whose portraits they had recognized. A defensive and harassed bookseller declared to a reporter that he was selling the novel "as a piece of literature and not as 'smut.' " After a week of furious gossip, the *Asheville Times* called the reaction of the town "sensational and tremendous."[8]

The bookstores soon sold out all the copies that were immediately available, and lending libraries enjoyed for a time an unequaled boom. "I had thought there might be a hundred people in that town who would read the book," Wolfe wrote in *The Story of a Novel*, "but if there were a hundred outside of the negro population, the blind, and the positively illiterate who did not read it, I do not know where they are."[9] Shocked by the growing scandal, the public library stood aside from the melee, and Wolfe's college play, *The Return of Buck Gavin*, was the only one of his writings that a patron could borrow

[8] *Asheville Times*, October 27, 1929.
[9] *The Story of a Novel*, 18.

until Scott Fitzgerald, angered because he did not find *Look Homeward, Angel* on the shelves six years after its publication, stalked out to a store and bought two copies, which he plunked down on the desk as a gift to the library. Impressed by a novel as perhaps they had never been before, ministers preached sermons on the subject.

Wolfe received anonymous letters, which he described in fiction, letters, and *The Story of a Novel.* They reviled, cursed, and threatened. There was a letter that threatened to kill him, and perhaps the post card he describes in *You Can't Go Home Again* is a literal quotation: "We'll kill you if you ever come back here. You know who."[10] There was another letter from an old lady who said she would not try to prevent a mob of lynchers from dragging Wolfe's "big overgroan karkus" through the streets.[11] When George Webber gets a similar letter in *You Can't Go Home Again,* the lady refers to his "monkyfied karkus."[12] There were also other kinds of reactions. In *The Marble Man's Wife,* Mrs. Julia Wolfe remarks on Cash Gudger's joy that he was in the book, and she quotes Dr. Arthur C. Ambler, who thought, "It's queer he didn't put me in the book."[13]

When there is much laying bare of human souls and their sins, weaknesses, and agonies, there must also inevitably be pathos, yet there is little indication that Wolfe had tried to ease much of the heartache. Some Ashevillians who were described have built up systems to explain their portraits in the *Angel* to themselves and to their acquaintances. One old gentleman whom Wolfe loved but whom he nevertheless presented

[10] *You Can't Go Home Again,* 336.
[11] *The Story of a Novel,* 18–19.
[12] *You Can't Go Home Again,* 336.
[13] Hayden Norwood, *The Marble Man's Wife* (New York, Charles Scribner's Sons, 1947), 119.

unfavorably in the book insists over and over, even to strangers, that "Tom didn't mean what he wrote about me. He didn't mean it. He didn't mean it." Perhaps he did not intend it, but Ashevillians thought he did, and that was the tragedy. Another insists that Wolfe had to have a villain, that he was chosen for that dubious role with his own consent, and that Wolfe even let him pick his own name, which he chose from *The Virginians*. Defense mechanisms such as these belie Edward C. Aswell's contention that the reaction to *Look Homeward, Angel* was due to Wolfe's laying bare "certain spiritual realities in American life."[14]

Surely no man has been so vulnerable to suits for libel and defamation of character; surely no town has ever felt itself so defamed and libeled. Strangely, however, despite all the opportunities, no Ashevillian has ever brought a suit for libel against Wolfe and the *Angel*. Indeed, although he continued throughout all his books to use factual and, sometimes, scandalous material, there has been only one libel suit against any of his works, and that was brought against "No Door," a short story set in the North and one of the most innocuous and innocent of all his works. This suit for one hundred and twenty-five thousand dollars, furthermore, was settled out of court by Scribner's, not because they feared losing it, but because it was so upsetting to Wolfe.[15] With sentiment against him as it was in 1929 and 1930, any one of a dozen persons—and perhaps more—could have sued and collected from him and Scribner's. Apparently many reasons account for his escaping this harass-

[14] Edward C. Aswell, "An Introduction to Thomas Wolfe," in Walser (ed.), *The Enigma of Thomas Wolfe*, 104; also printed in the *Saturday Review of Literature*, Vol. XXXI, No. 48 (November 27, 1948).

[15] Perkins, *Editor to Author*, 118. Another legal case involved threats of libel suits. See *Letters to His Mother*, 318–25.

ment: the love and respect for the Wolfe family and Wolfe himself must have been one significant factor; those who knew him and had some appreciation for his writing must have escaped temptation; finally, anyone who sued would have had to face notoriety and the publication of the real facts in Asheville and elsewhere. In this instance a suit for libel would have been an admission of infamy. No one sued.

While the battle was raging in Asheville, Wolfe himself, as the reader of *You Can't Go Home Again* knows, was spending his time alternating between shrinking from conflict and furiously hurling himself at his attackers. In this last novel he tells of a reporter's interviewing George Webber, who read the newspaper and then "sat down and wrote a scathing letter to the paper, but when he had finished he tore it up."[16] Like many other incidents in the novels, this one is based on reality; but like Wolfe's other letters and papers, this one was never torn up. Written between April and September, 1929, before the novel was even published, the letter begins with thanks "for your friendly and courteous invitation to contribute an article to your columns answering critics of my book, 'O, Lost.' " He declines because "the artist is neither a debater nor a propagandist. . . . If the Asheville critics of my work infer from this that I am anxious to avoid controversy, they are certainly right. But if, as I gather from several letters in your columns, they believe that my book is a 'bitter attack' against the town, the state, the South, they are certainly wrong."[17] He had known the storm was coming, but he had failed to grasp its magnitude and violence.

[16] *You Can't Go Home Again,* 124.

[17] *The Letters of Thomas Wolfe,* edited by Elizabeth Nowell (New York, Charles Scribner's Sons, 1956), 176. (Hereafter referred to as *Letters.*)

In the letters, *The Story of a Novel,* and *You Can't Go Home Again,* Wolfe recorded all the variety of emotions that beset him after he heard what his friends at home thought of his book. One chapter of the life of George Webber is given to a description of the emotional crises he experiences after his home town's violent reception of his first novel, *Home to Our Mountains.* That this account is autobiographical is seen from Wolfe's description of himself in *The Story of a Novel* as "spending my time consuming myself with anger, grief, and useless passion about the reception the book had had in my native town . . . ," and again he spoke of himself at this time as "absorbed in the emotional vortex which my first book had created. . . ."[18]

These were the calmer admissions after several years had eroded the ugliest places from his memory. In November of 1929, he had written his mother during the time of his own bitterness. He had expected, he quarreled, "as much kindness and fairness in the town of my birth as I would get from strangers," and he was "not grateful to people who try to make of my book a diary of family and town history."[19] At that early time he was still denying the literal use of the town in fiction and contending that pain and distress were not caused by the book, but by "a misunderstanding of the book's purpose."[20]

A substantial portion of Asheville's objections perhaps came from a naïve and honest objection to Wolfe's supposed poor taste in offenses against morality, and this sort of protest reinforced the cries of those who had been described. It was

[18] *The Story of a Novel,* 25–26.
[19] *Letters to His Mother,* 189.
[20] *Ibid.,* 190.

the old story of provincial and puritanical mores being offended by novels because they described fictitious sins. If an Ashevillian had written Defoe's *Moll Flanders*, the reactions would have been somewhat the same, although less intense. Here was at least one manifestation of what Wolfe struggled against in his own family and community when he was trying to become a writer. Anonymous letters of protest about the immorality of *Look Homeward, Angel* were written some years after its publication.

There had been material and financial crises in the collective lives of the pioneers who had struggled to build first houses and then palatial tourist resorts in the rugged mountains. Asheville had already undergone the terrible evils of a land boom and bust second only to the great Florida boom of the twenties, and just ahead there were the trials of the Great Depression and the bank failures and scandals that were worse than in most places. The greatest trial of all, however, was the publication of a novel, ordinarily a mild and transient event that may be significant only to the author. If the columnist's Colonel Blank Babers lived until 1929, he must often have yearned for books that were entirely fiction. Always, too, in the depths of the communal mind there was an even greater fear. The pen had not been stilled and the giant had not fallen. What would Thomas Wolfe write in his next history of the town? Even the reporters sometimes feared to speculate.

3. One Country, the First, the Last

"WHEN ARE YOU leaving, 'Gene?" the ghost of Ben Gant asks just before the end of *Look Homeward, Angel,* and Eugene answers, "Tomorrow." *Of Time and the River,* published six years after this first novel, opens with four people "standing together on the platform of the railway station of a town in the hills of western Catawba." Thus, less than twenty-four hours elapse between the action of Wolfe's first and second novels. This close connection in time well represents how the second continues the first in most respects. In *Look Homeward, Angel,* Wolfe described the life of Eugene Gant at home and in college until he left the South, and *Of Time and the River* continues the narrative of the same young man as he goes to the North, Harvard, and Europe, and finally to teach in a university in New York City. Eugene Gant in *Of Time and the River* is an older Wolfe than he was in the *Angel,* but he is the same Wolfe with the same background, family, home town, friends, and attitudes. When he spends time in Altamont, he again knows the people known by Gant and Wolfe in their home town.

Asheville had spat upon its own portrait, and Wolfe had writhed in the agony of guilt as well as persecution. Surely, if any young writer ever should have felt compelled to create a new and imaginary world of his own, Wolfe should have done so. In all his works there is little evidence that he could have peopled a town of his own imagination or created a hero who was not very much like himself in many respects. In the six years between the two books there was plenty of time to transpose his scene, but there is no substantial evidence of any serious effort to do it. That he could have made some change is shown by the shift from the Gant to the Webber cycle in his later books, but even these are so much based on the life of Wolfe that there is no indication that he was able to project his art into another person, time, and place. Wolfe may have thought that making Harvard, New York University, and Europe the major places of action would have relieved the bitterness; perhaps he did not care; perhaps he wished to create an entirely new hero and new characters but discovered that he could not; and it is not impossible that he did not realize how much he relied on fact. At any rate, he did not make the change. His use of the same Eugene Gant and Altamont enabled him to develop further the portrait of himself and the depiction of a Southern town and way of life. Had his works fragmented themselves over many times and scenes as the backgrounds of several distinctly different heroes, the over-all form and unity in all his writing would not exist. Even that change from Gant to Webber, after Wolfe had matured and changed publishers, perhaps weakened the total unity. Despite the harrowed feelings caused in Asheville and the consequent problems Wolfe had, building *Of Time and the River* on the foundation of *Look Homeward, Angel* has had fortunate artistic results.

There are, on the other hand, some indications that he did

attempt some changes to cushion the jolt to the town. Many characters in the first novel, most notably the Leonards, were omitted in the second. Some in *Look Homeward, Angel* appear with different names in *Of Time and the River*. In the first novel Wolfe described the newspaper publisher Mr. J. H. Brown and "the soles of his gouty feet" and "the veinous silken gloss of his slightly purple face." Altamont's newspaper publisher in *Of Time and the River* is similarly described; he is "bloated-looking," "gouty," and "satiny rosy," and has a "veinous and tender" face. This time, however, he is called Mr. Flood, a name not even remotely similar to J. H. Brown, used in the *Angel*. Perhaps Wolfe made this change because of antagonism toward this characterization in the first novel, but there were few editors in Asheville, and Mr. Jones could recognize his portrait about as well when he was called Flood as he could when he was called Brown. Again Wolfe seems to have disregarded opinion, and it is probable that when he wrote his second book, he simply did not check the names in *Look Homeward, Angel*. For this conclusion there is the additional evidence that the second portrait of the editor is more complete and detailed than the first.

Within the family of Wolfe and Gant there are a few interesting developments in fictitious nomenclature in the second book. In the first novel, the self-pitying W. O. Gant called on the memory of his first wife, Cynthia Gant (really Cynthia Wolfe, his second wife), "the gaunt tubercular spinstress whose life, it was said, his conduct had done nothing to prolong." In *Of Time and the River*, Eliza Gant describes seeing for the first time her future husband with his dying wife, but in this novel Wolfe calls her Lydia Gant. Avoiding the real name Cynthia and using the fictitious Lydia with the same *i* sound in the first syllable, the same *i-a* in the last, and the same kind of character is not concealment at all. It may indicate, however, a gentle wish for a little more obscurity. In Wolfe's naming of the family there is, on the other hand, a counter move that gives a better chance for recognition. Ollie Wolfe, the nephew of W. O. Wolfe, was Gilbert Gant in *Look Homeward, Angel,* but in *Of Time and the River,* Wolfe uses his real first name and calls him Ollie Gant. These two changes involving people in the family certainly reveal no consistent principles in the second novel.

Strangely, the Negro J. H. Jackson (owner of a "vegetable-stall" in *Look Homeward, Angel* and really B. J. Jackson, who sold vegetables in the city market) appears in Helen Gant's thoughts in the second book as "the nigger Jacken, the fruit and vegetable man." Mr. Rufus Z. Sorrells, owner of the Asheville Fish Company, is described in the first novel as Sorrell, "the fish and oyster man," and in *Of Time and the River* as Luther, "the fish man down in the market." Even Wolfe's careful working out of the change of Vanderbilt to Goulderbilt is tinkered with in his second book. Cornelia Vanderbilt, who found no place in the *Angel,* assumes the name of Virginia Willets. Apparently only utter disregard of consistency can account for this name, because later in the book Mrs. Vanderbilt again appears as Goulderbilt. The only logical conclusion from these inconsistencies seems to be that Wolfe in his second novel continued the methods he used in the first, but was so little worried about uniformity between minor details of the two books that he did not bother to check. A minor character, he seems to have thought, may add color and background under one name as effectively as under another. Yet this principle certainly contradicts his practice of making the name of a fictitious character similar to that of a real person. That his changing of the name of a character from one book to another is not unique among novelists may be seen by the studies of how William Faulkner's characters are at times inconsistent from one book to another.

Besides the reappearance of the family and the unchanged hero, many minor characters and places reappear in *Of Time and the River*. Such major places as the square of course remain unchanged, but even Lunn's Cove and Biltburn are in both books. Fagg Sluder, Mr. Jannadeau, the Tarkintons, Saul Gudger, and numerous other walk-on parts are acted by the same extras. Apparently the second book also has as characters many relatives of people who were described in the *Angel* but who do not reappear in the *River*. Emma Smathers may be a relative of Coston or of Dr. H. M. Smathers; Old Man Weaver perhaps is a member of the real Weaver family that was called Webster in the first book; Steve Patton, although not yet identified, is possibly a relative of the Pattons or Pastons in the first novel; Martha Patton and Annie Patton are similar; the Negro Joe Corpering has a name similar to that of Ella and May Corpering, who may have been one person with two names in *Look Homeward, Angel*.

Of Time and the River has new characters who were apparently not described and not related to characters in the *Angel*; but, although Wolfe continued to name ingeniously, he devised no new methods for this second book. Perhaps there were none to devise. The frantic young alcoholic Robert Weaver, who is from Altamont and who commits suicide after causing Gant considerable trouble in New York, was in life Henry Stevens, Mrs. Wolfe says in *The Marble Man's Wife*. Captain Bob Porter in the novel was probably Robert R. Porter, proprietor of the Asheville Tobacco Company. John Hugh William Macpherson Marriott seems to be John Francis Amherst Cecil, husband of Cornelia Vanderbilt and until his recent death the proprietor of the great Vanderbilt estate in Asheville. Dr. Ballard, who believes "that the souls of all the dear lost dead" go into his dogs, keeps in fiction the name that he had in life. The fireman Bickett is probably based on Wolfe's memories of the fireman Duckett. In naming Charlie Mascari, the fruit dealer, Wolfe gave him an Italian first name, too, and called him Tony Scarsati. Richmond Pearson became Junius Pearson. Fiction even lost some of the color of real names when Symcon Papas, proprietor of the New York Quick Lunch Restaurant, became merely "Mr. Pappas, Greek lunch-room proprietor."

Because *Of Time and the River* begins with Wolfe's leaving for Harvard, and because most of the years described in the novel were spent away from Asheville, he used fewer hometown characters in this second work than in the first novel. The total number of Northern, Southern, and foreign personalities reveals a canvas of similar extent. The use of real alien characters in the books belongs to another study, but although the methods were the same there was never so much bitterness in the North as there was in Asheville. Not belonging to the tradition and mores of a small Southern town, the aesthetes and cosmopolitans Wolfe knew at Harvard and in New York and Boston did not object so much. Indeed, Asheville itself has never opposed the *River* so violently as it did the *Angel.* Wolfe's separation from the town had its effect, and many a minor character is somewhat less vivid. Since there was less gossip, the researcher has a more difficult time in a study of Asheville as it appears in the second novel. If there is one single entirely fictitious person in this book, however, I do not know who it is. The many people whose prototypes I have not found still have local surnames. There are Curtises and Petries and Hartshorns and Pegrams and Martins and Pauls. Despite Wolfe's wrestling with the problems of autobiographical creation and despite his antagonism toward identifiers, *Of Time and the River* presents no evidence of attempts to create people of the mind who had not existed in a real time and place. When Wolfe wrote about North Carolina and the South, he had to return to Asheville and what he had known. Although this weakness is indicative of an amazing dependence on fact, it is perhaps the secret of Wolfe's art and understanding. Asheville had to suffer, but artistically the product is worth the price.

Even with the presence of factual descriptions of events and people in the novel, Wolfe might have shown a conciliatory attitude by avoiding great scandal, but there are two incidents told about characters that were almost as offensive as any of the objectionable parts of *Look Homeward, Angel.* Again he made no attempts to jumble characters and incidents so that they could not be recognized. Eugene Gant is entangled in an episode that reveals a growing objectivity and self-criticism of the author-hero. Gene starts to visit his sister at a little town in South Carolina; and twenty-five miles from Altamont, probably at Hendersonville, North Carolina, which is twenty-five miles from Asheville, he meets his drunken friend Robert Weaver. Joining him, Emmett Blake, and a man called Kitchin, he takes a wild alcoholic ride to Blackstone, South Carolina, which is the unpleasant name Wolfe gives to Greenville. The story of the arrest of these drunken lads, of their imprisonment in the jail, and of Eugene's infuriating and confused fight that results when he is put in a cell with a Negro is based on one of the many incidents that occurred because the adventurous and naïve Tom Wolfe was never one who knew how to stay out of trouble.

This event focuses not only on Eugene Gant but also on Emmett Blake, a wasted and reckless young man who, "time after time, after a hemorrhage of the lungs . . . had been taken to a sanitarium in an ambulance, and his death had seemed to be a matter of only a few hours. And time after time, he had come out again, and immediately started on another wild spree of women and corn whiskey with Robert and others of the same breed."[1] A nephew of George Blake, "the great Middle-Western manufacturer of cheap motor cars," this character was based on a man whom Wolfe knew, and he made the trip in life as in fiction and was arrested. But the terrible shame of his life is revealed by Blake himself when he pathetically screams threats against his wife and George Pentland and thus reveals his own cuckoldry. Here Wolfe was still willing to use autobiography and fact regardless of gossip and possible consequences.

The burly, brusque, drunken, and kindly Dr. Hugh McGuire in *Of Time and the River* is, along with W. O. Gant, one of Wolfe's best character creations and one of the most human and unique figures in American fiction. The evaluation of Wolfe's artistic achievement in the characterization is, of course, not dependent upon the sources that he found in Asheville, but it is also true that he did not create McGuire imaginatively. W. O. Gant's cancer and his long sickness and McGuire's treatment of Gant in his last days and McGuire's drunkenness and the other details of his life—these from all accounts

1 Thomas Wolfe, *Of Time and the River* (New York, Charles Scribner's Sons, 1935), 363.

are rather close to fact. There are, on the other hand, many scenes that Wolfe could not have observed, scenes created with dialogue and description so vivid that they have all the verisimilitude of good reporting.

On the morning when Gant is buried, someone discovers "a simple wreath of laurel leaves" signed "Hugh McGuire." And this stark description is followed by a stark statement: "For Hugh McGuire had been found dead at his desk at six o'clock that morning, the news had just spread through the town, and now, when people saw the wreath upon Gant's coffin, there was something in their hearts they could not utter."[2] This simple presentation of McGuire's death shows Wolfe at his best and reveals how he was beginning some development in imagination, in simplicity, and in irony. He could have uttered what the people were unable to express. McGuire's fatalism and his knowledge that he inevitably has to die, his defiant drinking in spite of its damage to his health—these result in a tragic irony that Wolfe might have expressed lyrically in his earlier work, but it is more effective as he wrote it, without giving the reader a single foreshadowing word about McGuire's death. The most significant factor here, however, is how Wolfe was not committed to fact. The truth is that the deaths of these two persons actually occurred nearly two years apart. This is chronological change deliberately designed for artistic effect; and it is especially moving because of the similarities in the lusts and the vitality of both Gant and McGuire, and because the unexpectedness of the doctor's death presents such a contrast to the long agony of Gant's dying.

"The Web of Earth," in *From Death to Morning,* gives a little more detail about McGuire's death, and here the interval

[2] *Ibid.,* 271.

between the deaths is closer to the fact. In the shorter work Mrs. Gant tells of how the doctor "had only a year longer to live himself, drinkin' himself to death, you know, just grievin' over the way that woman had acted,"[3] and this is a plain statement of what is only implied in *Of Time and the River.*

The excellent characterization of Helen Gant's tense personality as she violently reacts to the news that her father has died while she was asleep is Wolfe's artistic representation of his sister, Mrs. Mabel Wheaton, who was asleep when her father died. Perhaps the most effective passage in that long description of the death of stoneman Gant occurs when he falls asleep and dreams that he returns to his childhood home. The "tall flat slabs of marble with plain rounded tops" that Gant has carved and brought back from Baltimore is an imaginative but literal description of the Wolfe cemetery in Pennsylvania. The tombstones of Mr. Wolfe's sisters are described accurately as Tom Wolfe remembers them from the trip he made to his father's old home in 1932. Perhaps failure of memory accounts for his changing Sarah Ellen's name to Augusta. Huldah and Susan existed in fact as they do in fiction. Wolfe forgot ages, too. W. O. Gant dreams that Susan died in infancy, but Susan Wolfe lived over twenty years. Huldah, "who had died in childbirth while the war was on,"[4] really died in 1858 when she was thirteen years old, and it was Sarah Ellen who died in childbirth. Also, she was the wife of Eli Lents, not Jake Lentz, as Wolfe wrote.

Research has neither verified nor proved imaginary Willy Spangler, who has the "foolish witless face" and who asks Mr.

[3] Thomas Wolfe, *From Death to Morning* (New York, Charles Scribner's Sons, 1935), 256.

[4] *Of Time and the River,* 258.

Gant, "Ain't ye going to stay?"[5] Mr. Gant cannot stay, he says, for he's " 'meeting someone down the road' . . . why, where, with whom he did not know. . . ." Whether fact or fiction, this exploration of Gant's mind as he dreams of an idiot boy who evokes thoughts of the death Gant is hastening to encounter is one of Wolfe's simplest achievements of pathos.

The rural and pastoral tone in the description of Gant's nostalgic dream of his boyhood springs from a sensitive author's visit to his father's home, which is quite appropriate to the theme of a search for a father in *Of Time and the River*. Old Gant's longing for his former simple life is an emotion that reveals Wolfe's emotions on the visit of 1932. In his father's earth Wolfe found on that trip more understanding of his father's character, for the frame box-shaped house with a green roof and the outbuildings that would surround any farm had been the land of his father's dream at the moment of death.

Compared with Wolfe's treatment of the sordid family squabbles when Ben died in *Look Homeward, Angel*, the account of the death of old Gant presents a much more favorable view of the family. Eliza is praised by her dying husband in an awkward way: "Ah-h! your mother is a good cook, Helen. You're a good cook, too—but there's no one else can cook a chicken like your mother."[6] Somehow the old man communicates with his statement about the trivial chicken a significant idea that he has always needed to express, and the two reach an understanding while he is on his deathbed. Fumbling as the words are, Wolfe somehow suggests with them that there has been a sort of understanding all along the way, even in the turmoil. The family, and particularly Eliza, are portrayed more

[5] *Ibid.*, 259.
[6] *Ibid.*, 256.

nobly throughout *Of Time and the River*. Wolfe kept his deep sympathy and love for his mother mainly hidden in the first novel, but affections for her increasingly dominate his critical attitude in the later works, especially in this death scene and in "The Web of Earth." This is a significant mark of change and of his growing desire to return to those who had bred him.

Always in the novels Wolfe displays a keen admiration for his sister Helen Gant–Mabel Wheaton, who in fiction is distinguished by her habits of constantly repeating phrases and plucking her chin. In a wonderful passage in *Of Time and the River* he reveals her character clearer than anywhere else. When she sees the workingmen who visit her father in his last illness, she reflects on how she has always thought of them as "just working men" and becomes aware of her own excessive emphasis of social standards and attitudes. "Papa's not a working man —Papa is a *business* man," she tells herself, "a well thought of business man in this community." But Gant's symbolic hands cause her to realize that he is a stonecutter, and in characteristic sincerity, "going directly to old Alec Ramsay she grasped his blunt thick fingers . . . and greeted him in her large and spacious way."

Early in *Of Time and the River*, Eliza, Helen, and Eugene Gant are waiting for the train that will take him to Harvard. "They were on the point of parting; but they were talking about things to make talk," Mrs. Wolfe told Hayden Norwood. "There's lots of things that you don't know," Mrs. Gant tells Eugene; "you always thought you were the last—the youngest —didn't you?" This mysterious and unexplained enigma reveals Wolfe's uninhibited use, early in the novel, of the most intimate family lore. The veiled allusion is revealed on the last two pages of *The Marble Man's Wife*, when Mr. Norwood hears the story of "miscarriage under circumstances bordering on horror . . . a purple flower of tragic conflict and heroic fortitude." Wolfe's use of such a mysterious statement and his failure to develop it into any significance in plot or characterization reveal a weakness that may occur in autobiographical writing especially. To him it was clear; therefore, he forgot to explain it to the reader.

The two versions of the death of Hugh McGuire are indicative of a general tendency in Wolfe's writing. Often he retells a story in a different way and for different purposes. One of the most interesting of such twice-told tales is his description of Eugene's reading his play to Joel Pierce (really Olin Dows), when he visits the Pierce family in their mansion on the Hudson River.[7] The drama is Wolfe's own *Mannerhouse*, which was written during his Harvard days but not published until 1948. This incident gave him an opportunity to criticize objectively and under the guise of fiction his own writing about the South, and although he obviously still admired his early play, he did see its errors. He did not, however, tell the reader that Eugene Gant in his novel wrote about a boy called Eugene, as Wolfe had done; perhaps Wolfe did not wish the reader to see too easily that he was writing autobiographically about a character who wrote plays about himself using his own name. In many respects, the Eugene of the novel and the one of the play are the same character. Wolfe usually objected violently to any attempts to identify characters in his fiction, but young Eugene Gant freely confesses identification. In *Of Time and the River* he admits that the man named Porter in *Mannerhouse* was his Uncle William Pentland.

What little fiction there is in this part of *Of Time and the*

[7] *Of Time and the River*, 544–53.

River seems to spring from lapses of Wolfe's memory as he reproduced the plot of the play in fiction. Although he probably did not look at his manuscript while he was writing, he made no attempt at all to invent a fictitious plot or character for the hero of his novel to write about. In the drama the hero acts like Samson and pulls down the old family home, but in the novel the mighty Negro Tod is the destroyer. Racially and sociologically, such a change, of course, could have great significance, but since Tod in the novel is a loyal "gigantic faithful negro slave," acting for his master and thus the white race, no violence is done to the original theme. In both plays the idea is that the white realizes that the old order is being destroyed by newcomers of the poor white class. In the real play a minister preaches to slaves, quoting to them from Ephesians: "Servants, be obedient to thy masters, not only to the good and the gentle, but also to the forward." But the minister in *Of Time and the River* is of an entirely different mind; he urges "the man to see the crime of slavery, quoting the Scriptures with a telling aptness, urging him to repent, to join the life of town and church, to 'come to God.' " In this instance the version in the novel is better, because it strengthens the character of the slaveholder by his defiance of the church as well as human rights.

There are changes in incidents, some speeches are expanded, others are condensed, and speeches given to one character in the play are spoken by someone else in the novel. These two writings of the same story are excellent opportunities to see Wolfe's memory at work. He remembered content despite some slips, and the most memorable phrases, even of stage directions, appear in both. He could not reproduce exactly, nor did he try to. The bits of dialogue quoted in the novel do not follow the order of the conversations in the play. The mannerisms and traits of character in both are almost exactly the same. The facts of the prologue are remembered in general, but details, order, actions, and motivations are changed.

In addition to his recognition of autobiography in the play, he admits in *Of Time and the River* the influences on his drama of Chekhov, Rostand's *Cyrano de Bergerac*, and *Hamlet*. Through the use of these models he did impose a literary fashion on the play and give the action universal themes as well as his own rhetorical effects. Here may be the grounds of attack used by Ashevillians and the grounds Wolfe used in his own defense. He used "some of the powerful and imitable materials of life itself and of his own experience," he confesses in the novel. But Wolfe on the defensive, as he was in life more often than in fiction, was inclined to give greater emphasis to his own artistic accomplishments and adaptations.

One other incident in the Pierce home shows how Wolfe was concerned with the problem of the creative artist's description of his friends in fiction. An argument between his friend Joel and his friend's grandfather, Mr. Joel, "hinged particularly upon a certain book in which the writer had apparently made use of personal letters and private documents that people he knew, a woman chiefly, had written him."[8] Mr. Joel decides that no matter how great the work of the writer, he would "be forced to consider him a low cad." His son recites a list of great and guilty writers that Tom Wolfe himself must have made in his own defense—from Asheville, not from Mr. Joel—Rousseau, Byron, De Musset, and George Sand: "How wretched that stern judgment must have made Rousseau!" the skulking Wolfe exclaims. "What bitter news for Byron! What misery for De Musset!" Despite the sarcasm, what misery for Wolfe!

[8] *Ibid.*, 557.

This Southern boy's reading a play about the South to his aristocratic Northern friends on the Hudson brings into focus a new aspect of Wolfe's use of his home town and native region. No Southern writer has ever been more conscious of his origins and of the materials provided by his native town. In one of the exultant descriptions of America that Wolfe packed into *Of Time and the River,* there are long passages with paragraphs introduced by Whitman-like pointing lines that begin with the same words and phrases. Disregarding interspersed italicized passages, thirteen paragraphs begin with "It is the place of" or "It is the place where." There is a catalog of place names, beautiful girls, and other things from various geographical locations in America, but persons from Asheville provide the two most concrete and nostalgic of the italicized passages. These are Dr. Ballard and his dogs and the two Lipe girls, "*who lived in Biltburn by the river, and one of them was drowned in the flood. She was a cripple, and she wheeled herself along in a chair. She was strong as a bull.*"[9] This is a reappearance of that same flood that delayed the honeymoon of Hugh Barton and his wife in *Look Homeward, Angel,* and the principle of selection is dominant. Wolfe might have picked much more sensational details than those he used in this passage. The French Broad River went on such a rampage in 1916 that the Southern Railroad published a long book on the disaster, and for days the Asheville papers were filled with news of tragedies. One man trapped in a furniture store reportedly went insane before rescuers could reach him. The Lipe girls, to whom Wolfe devoted a short paragraph without troubling himself even to change their name, were the subjects of heroic newspaper stories. One of the most interesting aspects of this brief passage is its error in fact. Misses Nellie and Kathleen

[9] *Ibid.,* 157.

Lipe were reported dead, but they were saved, and for years afterward their names were listed in the city directory. One of them, indeed perhaps the one he wrote about, was alive after his death. Their father and two sisters named Walker, who lived with the Lipes, were lost in the flood. How Wolfe made this error in fact, especially since the flood occurred before he ever left Asheville, is impossible to determine. Perhaps he confused the Lipe and Walker girls, or perhaps he remembered the first report in the newspapers and conjoined it with the story about the strength of one of the girls. There are no evident aesthetic reasons for a change of this sort.

In *You Can't Go Home Again,* George Webber, with the help of Randy Shepperton, learns that it is all right to write about a horse thief, but he does not have to "give his street address. And there ain't no use in throwing in his telephone number, too."[10] Quoting this statement in his introduction to the same book, Edward Aswell writes also that "after a while there began to be a difference,"[11] and Wolfe "began to get away from his more literal interpretations of his experience." If ever he did, he had not reached that stage in *Of Time and the River.* There is, of course, less about the life of Asheville in his second novel, but not because of an increase in the powers of imagination. When he wrote of Asheville in this book, he still used scandals and names, street addresses, and telephone numbers of his native town. Indeed, the life of Tom Wolfe serves as an essential background for the fictitious accounts of Eugene Gant even when he is in the North and remembering the South. The foundation of the greatness of Wolfe's genius is largely attributable to what he knew of Asheville.

10 *You Can't Go Home Again,* 358.
11 Aswell, "Introduction" to *You Can't Go Home Again,* x.

4. *The Loom of Memory*

The growing cosmopolitanism of Wolfe's choice of subjects is revealed in his first collection of short stories and sketches, *From Death to Morning*. Of the fourteen stories in the volume, only six are set in the South. One of these has Virginia as its locale; and another, a story of the retirement of a railroad engineer, has such a vague setting that it could happen in any land. Wolfe's father is the only Ashevillian concretely described in "The Four Lost Men." The land and people of Wolfe's nativity are well represented in only the last three stories: "The Men of Old Catawba," "Circus at Dawn," and "The Web of Earth."

"The Men of Old Catawba" is an essay on the geography, races, and history of North Carolina and a character sketch of typical mountaineers of that state. Parallels between this selection and the introduction to the fragment *The Hills Beyond* suggest that Wolfe was perhaps trying here to begin a longer work that would have been a historical novel about his native state. Imagination and reality are related approximately in the way they are in his descriptions of Asheville. *Catawba* is actually the name of a county in North Carolina and of an Indian tribe; by adding *Old,* Wolfe derived a name very close to Old

Carolina or North Carolina; and the *Catawbas,* which he sometimes uses, is similar to Carolinas. He gives the area as more than 50,000 square miles, and it is really 52,712. The populations of whites and Negroes that he gives for this country of his mind are approximately those of his native state.

Wolfe's purpose, however, was much more ambitious than a brief encyclopedic sketch of North Carolina. By using typical people and subjects and by writing lyrically, he wished to give a poetic interpretation of the spirit of the earth and the people. Although he had been long from home, his native region still tenaciously retained his loyalty: "the land has a brooding presence that is immensely old and masculine, its spirit is rugged and rather desolate, yet it broods over its people with stern benevolence. The earth is a woman, but Old Catawba is a man."[1]

Then he tells imaginatively of the discovery of this man whose "brows are bowed with granite." A one-eyed Spaniard on his way north from the tropics is blown from his course to the shore of Old Catawba, "which stretched away with the immense indifference of nature into silence and wilderness." "But here," Wolfe writes, "a strange kind of exhilaration seizes the Spaniard," and he records in his journal that his men sang and laughed and began to be "marvellous merry."[2] They shouted jokes at the natives and "did laugh and caper as if they had been madde." Reaching land, they set up a flag claiming the land for the king of Spain and shot two or three among a crowd of Indians. "Thus, at one blast," writes Wolfe, "Christianity and government were established." They sacked the Indian village and recorded a derogatory criticism of the "wild and barbarous kind of race, full of bloudie ways."[3]

[1] *From Death to Morning,* 187. [2] *Ibid.,* 189. [3] *Ibid.,* 191.

This eight-page discussion of the plundering of the New World seems so authentic that the researcher who knows Wolfe's ways expects to find an account by an early traveler whose writing Wolfe has used with a few alterations. There are so many parallels in early tales about travel in North Carolina that the study is bewildering. Philip Amadas, who with Arthur Barlowe was one of Sir Walter Raleigh's adventurers in the New World, seems to have been in Wolfe's mind, but he was not one-eyed and the quotations are not lifted from Amadas and Barlowe's reports, or from Harriot's *A Brief and True Report of the New Found Land of Virginia,* or from any other such voyage that I have found. Apparently Wolfe did much reading in Hakluyt's *Voyages,* and he then wrote his own quotations, giving them the true spirit of Elizabethan writing and the ring of authenticity. No poor one-eyed Spaniard has been discovered in North Carolina's past. Probably Wolfe read Barlowe, Amadas, Harriot, and many other accounts of voyages in Hakluyt and created his own Spaniard, equipped with excerpts from an Elizabethan journal written by Tom Wolfe. The history of the North Carolina coast is simply infested with pirates; so he tied a patch over one of the eyes of his composite character to give him a *Treasure Island* look. This first explorer of the Carolina coastal area is, therefore, probably more fictional and imaginative than any of the inhabitants of Altamont. Wolfe could write fictitious history, even though the creation of an imaginary explorer was not the kind of fictionalizing that Asheville had been crying for.

"Circus at Dawn" seems to be one of those many extraneous sections lifted during the cutting of the huge manuscript of *Look Homeward, Angel.* Although it stands independent of other stories as a description of a small Southern town and a boy's love of "all the strange sounds and smells of the coming circus," it could also be inserted in its present form into the *Angel* without doing violence to the mood, continuity, or form of that work. Luke Gant's stuttering and Eugene's imagination in "Circus at Dawn" are indistinguishable from these traits in the first novel. One significance of the story, then, is its exemplification of the idea that the form of Wolfe's works is the pattern of his life. An interesting experiment would be the reworking of all the books into one chronological account, several thousand pages long, of the life of Wolfe-Gant-Webber.

"The Web of Earth," one of the best short stories Wolfe ever wrote, presents a technique that he had not used so extensively before. This novelette is a conglomeration of the memories of Mrs. Wolfe, or Eliza Gant, from her second year until the time when she sits in Wolfe's, or Gant's, New York apartment telling her son a tale composed of a thousand stories. The irony of Wolfe's life is seen in the juxtaposition of his mother's mountain-folk background against the sounds of ships in the New York harbor. Near the beginning and at the end of "The Web of Earth" she hears the ships and begs him to come home.

Beginning in midsentence and ending with a question, this story is in technique a stream of disorganized conversation, derived from a garrulous mountaineer's endless gossip, superstition, and folklore. The method of narrative apparently stems directly from Wolfe's ability to reproduce his mother's manner of telling stories about her memories. She begins to tell a story of voices in the year the locusts came, "Says, 'Two . . . Two,' says, 'Twenty . . . Twenty,' " but in the ninety-four-page story there are thousands of bypaths, and often the son has to remind his mother of the basic thread of narrative. The sole reason for many dead-end sections of the narrative seems to be Eliza's proving the excellence of her memory. One of Mrs. Wolfe's friends once asked her if she had written the story and then said, "It talks just like you."[4] This folk art must belong to his mother, but the difference between *The Marble Man's Wife* and "The Web of Earth" is proof of his refinement and alteration of the facts.

The description of the methods of the story seems to indicate a degree of complication that is not actually present. Folk humor, folk digression, the character of the lady who tells the tale, the mountaineer's pungent and sensuous description of the concrete facts of existence, and the background for both character and narrative that is given in the digressions—all these make this a tale of the earth; and the web of the narrative is such that an old-fashioned mountaineer who heard the story read aloud would not consider it at all unusual. This story, in short, is of the bone and sinew of the South, and it is one of the very best aspects of Wolfe's art. Realizing that his mother could not fail to see herself in the story, he wrote her that he considered it "an honorable tribute to her courage, strength, and character."[5] He was worried about his mother's being annoyed by questions, and he declared that he had "not the slightest interest in printing local gossip or digging up old scandals."

But he did dig up old scandals, his mother did object, and newspaper reporters printed an article about her unpleasant memories and her fears that relatives of the deceased people Wolfe wrote about would be offended. The central thread of

[4] Julia Elizabeth Wolfe, "*Look Homeward, Angel,*" transcribed by Ruth Davis, *Saturday Review of Literature*, Vol. XXIX, No. 1 (January 5, 1946), 31.
[5] *Letters to His Mother*, 221.

the narrative deals with the extremes of mountaineer violence, murder, plots, escapes, and a visit to the Gant home to get shoes to aid in escape. For sixty pages there are allusions to the main crime and its consequences, but Eliza does not become really concerned with this episode until the last third of "The Web of Earth"; and even then the narrative is entirely out of chronological order, so that it must be rearranged in any comparison of what happened in life with what Wolfe or his mother told.

The initial violence begins when two men "walked in to that mica mine on Saturday afternoon when they were payin' off, and they were spoilin' for a fight."[6] After abusing the paymaster, one of them tells a would-be mediator, " 'Why, damn you,' he says, 'I never did like your face noway.' " When the scorned man gives up and turns to walk away, one of the ruffians shoots him through the back of the head just to prove that he is a good shot. It is a simply told tale of cruelty and primitive alcoholic violence, but it is only partly true. In the 1880's, Wates Anderson and Ed Ray (spelled *Wray* in some accounts) invested in a mica mine in mountainous Mitchell County, but the owners of the mine refused to give up control to the two cousins, and in a gun battle Anderson and Ray killed three of the operators of the mine.[7] Wolfe follows the facts even to the number of dead, but the significant change is the omission of the motive: "There was no excuse, no provocation as far as I can see," Eliza says, "they were *simply out to kill*. . . ."[8]

After the men are put in jail, several incidents arouse the suspicions of Eliza Gant. A hardened defense attorney, Mel

[6] *From Death to Morning*, 280.
[7] *Charlotte Observer*, November 12, 1933.
[8] *From Death to Morning*, 281.

Porter, shows excessive worry over his failure to get them acquitted.[9] Dock Hensley will have the duty of executing the murderers, even though they are his close friends, but he explains to Mr. Gant by saying that "they'd rather have me do it than some stranger." And after all, that is why the people elected him, and he would think no more about hanging them than he would about wringing a chicken's neck.[10] Just in case Mr. Gant wishes to attend the public ceremony, Hensley offers him two tickets.[11]

Hensley's brutality toward his friends extends even further. Once Reese McLendon, also his close friend, was arrested for drunkenness and disturbing the peace, but in the jail "he got to making so much noise that they had to take him out of the cell." Because he howled so loudly, he was put in the dungeon. When Hensley went down to quiet him, McLendon "tried to brain him with the horseshoe" that he had found. But Hensley hit him so hard and so many times that "the whole side of his head was bashed into jelly and he lay there welterin' in his blood."

In this instance Wolfe has worked one of Asheville's most sensational slayings into Eliza's story of Dock Hensley. Reese McLendon is the somewhat fictitious name for a real ruffian who was killed by the chief of police more than ten years after Ray and Anderson escaped. Despite Wolfe's utter disregard of historical time in having this incident occur some years before the escape, most of the details in the story are accurately based on this affray. Like McLendon, the real villain was arrested for "being drunk and disorderly on the streets." "The

[9] *Ibid.*, 226.
[10] *Ibid.*, 277.
[11] *Ibid.*, 271.

fatal encounter," wrote the reporter for the *Asheville Citizen,* "took place in the gloomy half light of the basement of city hall, just in front of the dungeon door. It was a life and death struggle between two powerful men—the one vicious and maddened by drink, the other in the discharge of his official duty and the defense of his life. The conflict was short, terrible, silent."[12] There is, however, a curious change that Wolfe made in the weapons. McLendon's horseshoe, according to the *Citizen,* was in fact "a piece of wagon tire some 18 inches long," certainly more dangerous. The chief of police in life found a pick handle and hit the prisoner, who at that moment still had his weapon and was trying to get in his own lick; but in fiction the slain man is defenseless, because Wolfe has the policeman take the horseshoe away from him and kill him with it. Although McLendon is killed immediately, the real villain lived for about three hours after the fight was over. This desperado is described vividly even in the *Citizen's* notice of his death: "He was a man of great strength, and was dreaded by everyone while he was intoxicated. His body, it is said, was literally covered with scars received in his numerous broils."

Mrs. Wolfe's and her son's memories were too exact and the killing is too well remembered for them to forget and change the story as it has been changed. Perhaps, also, the tendency of the paper to support the law explains the difference between the journalistic account and Wolfe's story. Besides changing the weapon, Wolfe made the officer the villain and the prisoner simply a drunken bully. Brutal as the crime was in real life, Wolfe in "The Web of Earth" has made it more brutal and inexcusable than it was in fact. Prosecuting Attorney Zeb Pentland in the fiction brings Hensley to trial and describes

[12] *Asheville Citizen.*

him "as he sits there before you! . . . cowerin' and tremblin' with the mark of Cain upon his brow and with his hands red with the blood of all his victims!" Actually, a coroner's jury found a verdict of self-defense and acquitted the policeman on the morning after the slaying.

Wolfe used other methods of exaggeration. Asheville today remembers no law-enforcement officer who killed eighteen men, as Wolfe said Hensley did. In "The Web of Earth," W. O. and Eliza Gant eat dinner with Hensley and find that he uses for a sugar bowl "the skull of a nigger he had shot and killed . . . with the top of the skull sawed off to make a lid and a place in the forehead for the sugar to pour out where the bullet hole was." Today in Asheville there are still stories of such misuse of skulls, but they are so legendary that it has been impossible to trace their origins to the fact. It seems most likely that Wolfe knew these tales and saw an excellent chance to increase the horror and atrocities in the already exaggerated novelette.

That Wolfe was interested in making the story of "The Web of Earth" as violent as possible is shown by the violation of historical facts in many instances. The sheriff who killed the prisoner, who became conscience stricken, and who finally committed suicide was not involved in the Ray-Anderson case at all. The sheriff who is listed in one source as being in office during the trial died a natural death.[13] Wolfe liked to pride himself on his representation of life, but life in this instance was less effective than it was after transposition and violation of historical truth. There were at least two virtues in the change: it made a better story, and Asheville would have a harder time remembering and discovering the facts.

[13] George A. Digges, Jr., *Historical Facts Concerning Buncombe County Government* (Asheville, 1935).

Wolfe, however, was not content with the facts of the lives of just two sheriffs as he created the life of this composite character described by Eliza Gant. John Rand, the jailer, is found tied up and suffering from no mark of violence upon him just after the escape of the two murderers. The story, as told by Miss Eliza, is that Rand "had been fixed, as the sayin' goes, to let them make their getaway."[14] Then in less than six months Rand buys a plumbing shop "with a stock that must have cost him thousands of dollars."[15] Arthur, in his *Western North Carolina: A History (from 1730 to 1913)*, writes a paragraph on this series of episodes and states the following: "On the night of July 3, 1885, these men with an ax broke a hole in the brick wall of the jail, and escaped. They had forced the sheriff, the late J. R. Rich, and J. D. Henderson, the jailer, into the cage in which the prisoners were confined, when they were tied and gagged. The military company was called out to recapture the prisoners, but without result. Proceedings were instituted against Rich and Henderson for suffering these escapes, but both were acquitted in January, 1886."[16] It was the sheriff, not the jailer, who became a plumber. In the city directory of 1887, J. R. Rich is listed as a tinner for the first time; in 1896, he is called a plumber. Now the cause of Mrs. Wolfe's displeasure at "The Web of Earth" is obvious. Her son took the most sensational elements of many of her stories and wove them together in a web of narrative modeled after her manner of conversing, and this stark account of the escapades of the law in a small mountain town is dramatized by combination,

[14] *From Death to Morning*, 278.

[15] *Ibid.*, 279.

[16] John Preston Arthur, *Western North Carolina: A History (from 1730 to 1930)* (Raleigh, Edwards and Broughton Printing Company, 1914), 305–306.

exaggeration, and changes of incidents. Many of those modern readers who knew the tales must have felt some of the old violence of their mountaineer ancestors stir within them.

The lives of the men who escaped from the jail are as pathetic and dramatic as any legend of the Carolina hills. In the darkness of the night of their escape, one of them comes to the Gant house while W. O. has gone to see what the commotion is about. Miss Eliza meets the fleeing prisoner alone, gives him a pair of shoes for his bare and bleeding feet (no one in Altamont besides Mr. Gant wears shoes large enough to fit him), and takes his gun away from him so that he cannot kill again. Once Mrs. Wolfe told John Skally Terry's class at New York University the basis of this story, and for once a Wolfe forgot! She told the students that the two men were robbers instead of murderers. Two, not one, actually came, she said. Wolfe changed it to one in order to develop further the symbolism of his story. Mrs. Wolfe met them alone, "went to the closet [with one of them] and took out a pair of shoes practically new and handed them to him," and took the pistol.[17] Not an incident in her packed description of the episode and of her conversation with the murderers varies from what her son wrote, with the single exception of her statement that the men were robbers.

In *The Marble Man's Wife*, however, Mrs. Wolfe told Hayden Norwood an entirely different and contradictory version about the same incident, yet that work was published little more than a year after she talked to Mr. Terry's class. Honest and straightforward as the Wolfes always are, Mrs. Wolfe said that the murderers were Ed Ray and "Waites" [*sic*]

[17] Julia Wolfe, "*Look Homeward, Angel,*" transcribed by Ruth Davis, *Saturday Review of Literature*, Vol. XXIX, No. 1 (January 5, 1946), 31.

Anderson and that her son told about facts up to the point where the murderers came to her house: "But that was fiction about the murderer coming here. I knew him, though, and the only good thing I found in that story was that Ed Ray or Ed Mears came and said he came because he could trust me—came to get a pair of shoes. That is the fiction that I went to the closet and gave him a practically new pair of shoes."[18] Apparently this is a trick and fallacy of memory, but how many of Wolfe's changes of facts should be ascribed to the unintentional alteration of folk gossip or tales not even the revived dead could exactly say.

Having escaped, the character Ed Mears flees to Colorado, followed by his wife, who leaves him after a year or so because he is going crazy and "screaming and raving that the spirits of the dead men he had killed had come back from the grave to haunt and torment him."[19] Sent back to North Carolina by her father, she gets a divorce and marries the lawyer who handled the case. Then Dock Hensley, sent west to get a murderer, meets Ed Mears, who "looked like a dead man." Thinking Hensley has been sent to get him, Mears surrenders; but when he learns that he is not the wanted man, he sends by Hensley a threatening letter to Cash Jeter, the husband of Mears's former wife: "You can set your house in order and get ready for me because I'm coming back." But he never gets back; "The story went that he got killed in a saloon in Mexico."

The real Wates Anderson settled in Nogales, Arizona Territory, and became a special officer with the alias of Charles Hood, who guarded trains for Wells, Fargo and Company after he was appointed United States deputy marshal of Arizona.

[18] Norwood, *The Marble Man's Wife*, 105–106.
[19] *From Death to Morning*, 291.

Later he held several official positions for the territory, entered the United States customs service, became deputy sheriff of Cochise County, and won fame as a capturer of desperadoes. For more than twenty years Wates Anderson was known as officer of the law Charles Hood. The last years of his life he spent in an unsuccessful attempt to get a pardon so that he could return to his native state and see his friends and relatives. "You must remember," he wrote his cousin in North Carolina, "the time that C—— B and N—— went to Raleigh to see the governor for me. The governor promised B—— that he would grant their request if J—— P—— would only have a negro postmaster at Wilmington, N. C., removed from office, and P—— would not do so. . . . Let me know where P—— is and what he is doing. I don't think there is anything too low for him to do against me." "It is to be noted," adds the discreet feature writer who published this correspondence in a newspaper, "that P—— had married into Anderson's family but was of a different political party."[20] From these initials and blanks it is easy to discover the name of the senator from North Carolina who was a Republican. Thus, Wolfe's story is not only close to truth but is, in this instance, truth that newspapers do not wish to print.

The story of Anderson remained mostly legend until E. L. Carter discovered his old letters and published a story in the *Charlotte Observer* in November, 1933. Wolfe's reliance on legend and family lore is shown by his printing the story in *Scribner's Magazine* in July, 1932, over a year before the facts of Anderson's life became public information. Mrs. Wolfe's lack of knowledge about Anderson may have led to her son's speculation about the criminal and desperate life and death of

[20] *Charlotte Observer*, November 12, 1933.

the fugitive, but possibly he did hear the facts and cho alter the ending of the true story. Anderson fought witl American troops during the troubles with Mexico before World War I, and fever he contracted there killed him in less than a year after he was discharged. This would have been an ignoble end for Tom Wolfe's desperado, and the desperate years and violent death of Ed Mears in a saloon brawl are much more in keeping with the violence described by Eliza Gant throughout "The Web of Earth."

This novelette is a web of violence, fact, and memory. The tangled narrative seems to be constructed from an author's ability to transcribe his mother's conversation, and the disorganization itself is an art that makes the tale more folkish as well as different from the swelling lyrical passages of the other books. The numerous attempts of later scholars and reporters to transcribe the talk of members of the Wolfe clan prove in every instance Tom Wolfe's superiority over the uncreative journalistic tribe, and even a personal talk with a member of the family reveals his supreme selection of manner and material. "The Web of Earth" is a compression of a lifetime of tales and gossip. Although Wolfe in *Look Homeward, Angel* turned to James Joyce to find a method to describe his father's thoughts (and old Gant's mind well fits that sort of style), he returned mainly to his mountaineer origins to find the method for the tales of Buncombe and Yancey counties. In the later stories he used this method more and more, especially in the short stories of *The Hills Beyond.*

The development of the symbols of superstition in "The Web of Earth" is one of the most artistic aspects of the narrative, and again it is based on his mother's manner of conversation. Mrs. Wolfe's own symbolism, as it is revealed in transcriptions of her talk, is primitive and omnipresent. She had an instinctive love of symbol characteristic of the innate poetry of the primitive mountaineer race. The first thing she told the class at New York University was her age, but she chose to give it in a riddle of numbers: "I'm three times six, four times seven, two times nine, eleven and eleven."[21] After Wolfe's death she told her daughter that her October children were buried: Leslie, Grover, Ben, and Tom. All four were born in October, and Ben died in that month. The habit of a repeated refrain, which is so ever recurrent in the Wolfe books, comes perhaps from the members of his family. Twice Mrs. Wolfe told in print the basis of the "Two-Two" and "Twenty-Twenty" symbols in "The Web of Earth."[22] "Just imagine somebody putting their arm around your shoulders. I hadn't been in bed five minutes, thinking how long could I go on. They put their arm around me and sort of squeezed me and whispered in this ear, 'Two-two,' and over at that window another voice called out loud, 'Twenty-Twenty.' " She believed that they predicted her death in two weeks or twenty days, but in twenty days she gave birth to two babies, Grover and Ben Wolfe.

This simple tale of superstition became more complicated when Wolfe told it in "The Web of Earth." No large brood of the seventeen-year locusts came in 1892, when Ben and Grover were born, or in 1885, when Anderson and Ray escaped. They came in 1889. The days are wrong, too. Mrs. Gant heard the voices on September 27, but Grover and Ben were born October 27, thirty days later instead of twenty. There can

[21] Julia Wolfe, "*Look Homeward, Angel*," transcribed by Ruth Davis, *Saturday Review of Literature*, Vol. XXIX, No. 1 (January 5, 1946), 13.
[22] *Ibid.*, 31; Norwood, *The Marble Man's Wife*, 104.

hardly be an artistic reason for the change Wolfe made here. Mrs. Wolfe must have dated some other event by the locusts, but because "the year the locusts came" has a lyric sound, Wolfe added this ominous phrase to the other symbols. The criminals escaped July 3, 1885, four years before the locusts came, seven years before the twins were born, and nearly three months before the time of the year when Eliza heard the voices.

"You must have dreamed it,"[23] Mr. Gant tells Eliza, and Mr. Wolfe had said, "You were dreaming."[24] Whereas Mrs. Wolfe said she thought no more about the voices after she heard them, Eliza speculates on all kinds of meanings for them. When she realizes the murderers are coming to her house, she decides that the voices must have meant that the two escapees would be at her house in twenty minutes.[25] But Eliza discovers the same meaning of the voices that Mrs. Wolfe did: "*Twenty* days later from that evening that Ed Mears came there to our house, to the minute, at twenty minutes to ten o'clock on the seventeenth day of October, *twins* were born. . . ."[26]

It is impossible to examine in minute detail all the factual bases of the story told by Eliza Gant. There is little reason to suspect that any portion is strictly fiction. The narrative alludes to thousands of details that are also mentioned in other works, and in most instances consistency proves Wolfe's use of fact more than it proves any consistency in his imagination. Eliza tells several stories about her family, but one of particular interest deals with old Bill Pentland, Eugene's great-grandfather, who sends for his son Sam to come to see him. " 'I never felt better, but I'm not going to be here with you much longer,'

23 *From Death to Morning,* 212.
24 Norwood, *The Marble Man's Wife,* 104.
25 *From Death to Morning,* 284.
26 *Ibid.,* 303.

he says, 'I've made up my mind it's time to die, Sam, and I want to put my house in order before I go.'" "Ten minutes after six tomorrow afternoon" is the time he sets for his death. Old Bill and his son talk all night and all the next day. "On the stroke of six, he turned to Sam and said, 'Get ready, Sam,' and at ten minutes after six to the dot, he looked at him again and said, 'Good-bye, Sam: it's my time, I'm going, son,' and he turned his face to the wall, sir, and *died*. . . ."[27] To summarize this story as Mrs. Wolfe told it to Hayden Norwood would be to tell the same story again with the same names, time, and incident.[28] Yet in several respects Wolfe surpasses Norwood, who could not sympathize with, understand, and reproduce Mrs. Wolfe's character, background, and culture. The sparse tales that she tells in *The Marble Man's Wife* are without the adornment, intricacy, and detail that Wolfe achieves. Above all, the poetry of a simple folk life is present in the fictitious account as Wolfe saw it and created it. And the tales in the journalistic version, without the poetry of elemental passions and expressions, are more sordid. This comparison helps one to see how truly he based his art on the folk art of those he had known in the mountains of the South.

Wolfe's quantitative use of the South is small in *From Death to Morning*, except in "The Men of Old Catawba" and "The Web of Earth." But in a study of Wolfe and the South there is perhaps no more significant point in his development. Artistically there is a turning back. His region is more primitive and rural in "The Web of Earth" than it was in *Look Homeward, Angel*, and the form and style are quite different

[27] *Ibid.*, 221.

[28] Norwood, *The Marble Man's Wife*, 100. See also Julia Wolfe, "*Look Homeward, Angel*," transcribed by Ruth Davis, *Saturday Review of Literature*, Vol. XXIX, No. 1 (January 5, 1946), 14, 31.

from what they were before. The South and the Gants and the Wolfes are present, not only with more details in this work, but also in a different and varied form. Wolfe's achievement here is the conveying of an interesting subject matter in a most appropriate way. No author has ever better represented the primitive and simple tales of the Southern mountaineer.

5. *The Web of Youth Again*

JUST BEFORE Thomas Wolfe left Asheville for the last time, in 1937, he took one of the most momentous steps of his career. Impulsively making a decision to complete immediately his plan to leave Scribner's and to give up the editorial advice of Maxwell Perkins, late one evening he called many prominent New York publishers. Decsriptions of those calls indicate that he used the approach direct. "My name is Wolfe. Would you be interested in publishing me?" was the beginning of each conversation. To his dismay, every publisher he called declined, and the negative results of those abrupt negotiations are reported to have thrown him into one of his extremely despondent moods. He did not realize that his tempestuous manners led the publishers to believe that they were being called as a joke or by a drunk. This change, however, was eventually accomplished when Wolfe forsook Scribner's and Perkins and went to Harpers, who offered Edward C. Aswell as editor.

Wolfe's telephone calls and the change of publishers were probably the direct result of adverse criticism and charges that Perkins, not Wolfe, was the true creative genius of Wolfe's works. In the person of Monk Webber, Wolfe tried to explain his move away from his first editor on philosophical grounds, but he made this decision to prove his independence. Even after the change there remained the problem of Perkins' influence. Since Wolfe had written about his home town, his family, and the colleges that he had attended and at which he had taught, and since the characters in these works had been continued from one book to another, the detractors could maintain that, if Wolfe continued to write about the same subjects, he was only developing further what he had already begun with Perkins' help. Reasoning of this sort led him to counter not only by changing publishers but also by attempting to change his hero, the hero's family and home town, and all the circumstances of his life. When he began writing about his new hero is not known, but the two posthumous novels devoted to Webber contain many passages from short stories that were closely related to the Gant cycle and that probably could have been worked into novels about Eugene Gant if the change had never been made.

At least he attempted such a new beginning, and it in some respects led him farther from the life on which he had based his early books. When he started anew, he was faced with the problem of developing another hero and an adequate background for him. To take Monk Webber and write about his career from the point where Wolfe had ended the description of his own life in *Of Time and the River* would have been an admission that Monk Webber was Eugene Gant with a different name. Wolfe was therefore faced with the problem of creating a childhood and youth for Webber, and thus he had to write again about the period of his life that he had already treated in *Look Homeward, Angel.* Apparently he never thought of rejecting autobiography and taking a character already mature, or even one of a nature considerably different from his own and Gant's.

As the solution to these problems, *The Web and the Rock* is a book of clear divisions. The first 170 pages are explicitly the narrative of the early life of Monk Webber in Libya Hill and implicitly a variation of the lives of Eugene Gant in Altamont and Tom Wolfe in Asheville. Only about 50 pages are given to Webber at Pine Rock College, a subject anticipated by Wolfe's life at Chapel Hill and Eugene Gant's at Pulpit Hill. After one-third of the novel is completed, Webber is in New York, where Gant was when his creator had blotted the last line on his short and stormy life. Webber spends a year or so living with some of his college friends from the South and then moves into a little room in downtown New York, where he begins trying to write. After about 300 pages, Webber is found returning from Europe on a ship that is also bearing Mrs. Esther Jack to America. Eugene Gant met the same lady, also called Esther, on a ship in the last pages of *Of Time and the River,* and Monk Webber rides the same boat and completes the courtship of the woman whom Eugene loved.

At this point in the novel Wolfe completed his overlapping of the earlier novels and was ready to plunge ahead into new realms of his autobiography and the career of his one hero with two different names. There are, of course, physical differences between the heroes. (Eugene was tall and huge like Wolfe) but Monk is barrel-chested and short, and his long arms give him a simian appearance. In personality, character, and basic urges, however, Webber is as clearly Wolfe as was his predecessor Gant. Although some critics have deplored this doubling back and covering of the same material, it has had some fortunate results. Huge portions of manuscript had been lifted from

Look Homeward, Angel and stored in those famous packing cases that Wolfe kept filled with his writings. The development of the life of Webber gave him an opportunity to use some of that material and to write again the life of a young boy in a small Southern town. The loss of the first part of *The Web and the Rock* would be a great one, for Wolfe never wrote better on any subject than he did on his own childhood in Asheville. The second writing about this period proves that the materials were virtually inexhaustible. Except for the briefer treatment of members of the family, there seems to be little loss of detail and no decline in his ability to characterize.

The change from Altamont to Libya Hill was not as complete as most readers suppose it to be and perhaps not even as extensive as Wolfe himself thought it was. Many of the characters from his life and the first books reappear in different but recognizable personalities, and many of the members of the Westall and Wolfe families are obviously used in this new fiction. John Webber, a Pennsylvania Dutchman, comes to Libya Hill on page 1 of the novel just as W. O. Gant, the half-English, half-Dutch Pennsylvanian, arrived in Altamont in the early pages of the *Angel* and as W. O. Wolfe, a Pennsylvanian, had come to Asheville in life. Mr. Webber, the brick mason, sees life in parables of brick and stone, and he labors with his hands as Mr. Gant and Mr. Wolfe did. Detailing the parallels of the lives of these three men becomes in time a fruitless occupation. There are more similarities than contrasts to be found.

In 1885 or 1886, John Webber marries Amelia Joyner, a new character who is derived from both Eliza Gant and Cynthia Gant. They remain childless for fifteen years, until 1900, when the hero George Webber is born. In 1908, they separate because of a young woman named Bartlett with whom Webber has an affair. That this had a degree of authenticity in Mr. Wolfe's life is shown by the fact that Wolfe had already told a similar tale about Gant and Eller Beals in "The Web of Earth." Even the separation is based on family background. Eliza Gant set up her own home and left Mr. Gant at his place on Woodson Street when she established the Dixieland boarding-house during Eugene's childhood, and always Eugene (as well as Tom) was torn between the two homes that he had.

Although the Webbers have only one child and Amelia dies soon after the separation, some of the members of Wolfe's immediate family do appear in other roles in the last novels. In addition to being a prototype of Amelia Joyner, Mrs. Wolfe is also Aunt Maw, who rears George Webber after the death of his mother. Randy Shepperton is the new fictitious representation of Wolfe's brother-in-law, Ralph Wheaton, who was called Hugh Barton in the Gant cycle; but Randy is much more of a composite character than Hugh was. Some of the things he does in the novel were in fact the actions of Fred Wolfe, Mabel Wheaton, and others. Although Wolfe did not know Mr. Wheaton until a short time before he married into the family, Randy grows up in Asheville and goes to college with George Webber. In both Barton and Shepperton, the *t-o-n* ending of the name is preserved, and the Randy of *The Web and the Rock* is closer to the name *Ralph* than Hugh is. Despite these carry-overs of some of the Wolfes, the role of the immediate family is much less important in the Webber cycle than it was in the early books.

Many of the new characters are not really new at all. Their connection with the early books is often so obvious that a student of parallels between the works promptly recognizes not only the characters but also the names. There is evidence that the change from one cycle to another started before Wolfe finished *Of Time and the River* and that sometimes he still wrote of Altamont after he had started a new book and ostensibly given up Altamont for Libya Hill entirely. Cornelia Vanderbilt, for example, was a Willets in *Of Time and the River,* although the rest of the Vanderbilts were called Goulderbilt; yet George Vanderbilt also acquires the family name of Willets in *The Web and the Rock.* The long name for John Francis Amherst Cecil in *Of Time and the River,* John Hugh William Macpherson Marriott, was merely shortened to Hugh Macpherson in the Webber cycle; but when the passage about him was first printed as a short story in the *Saturday Evening Post,* the same man was called Hugh McNair. Mike Fogarty, the friend of W. O. Gant, is obviously the same person as Mack Hagerty, John Webber's friend. The saloonkeeper Tim O'Connell represents a minor change from Tim O'Donnel in the first novel as well as from John O'Donnel in real life. Lunn's Cove is the same except that Wolfe omitted *Lunn's* and called it only the Cove. *Double Day* in the *Angel* merely became one word instead of two. Ernest Peagram in life became Ernest Pegram in the first novel and Ernest Pennock in *The Web and the Rock.*

There are many other indications of relationships between names and people in *The Web and the Rock* and those in *Look Homeward, Angel,* but although these all seem to give a feel of continuity to the Webber books, the evidence is slight, and the connection is so tenuous that these could not be proved. A few illustrations will serve. The policeman Mr. Matthews may be a changed Big Bill Messler or old Bill Smathers; Rheinhart seems to reappear in Rheinhardt; Sawyer's grocery store is comparable with both Garrett's Grocery and Jim Sawyer of the first novel; Zebulon Pentland of *From Death to Morning* is perhaps Zebulon N. Meekins of *The Web and the Rock;* the Tarkintons probably reappear as Higginsons; there are Redmonds in stories about Webber and Gant.

Many characters who are presented for the first time in this book are as obviously based on life as were those in *Look Homeward, Angel.* The list of characters used in Wolfe's first novel is so extensive that one would assume at first glance that he had used every character whom he could remember, list, and describe. From imagination and memory together he added in *The Web and the Rock* at least sixty-four local characters whom he had not used before. These include twenty-eight with known prototypes, and probably most of the persons in this fourth book are based on reality. Some of the fictitious characters, indeed, are derived from as many as three real persons. Edward Aswell has maintained that Wolfe created more people from his imagination in the later books and that Nebraska Crane is entirely a creature of the imagination, but characters distinct in every respect from real Asheville persons and incidents are certainly few. Nearly every surname in *The Web and the Rock* appears also in the city directories. Nearly all the places mentioned are very easily identified in the directories or newspapers, or simply by studying the places in the town.

Wolfe had the opportunity to study directories of other towns, to make complete changes in the names, and thus to avoid some of the antagonism created by his previous books; but there is little indication that he tried to avoid giving his new characters names similar to those of real people in Asheville. The closeness of fiction to life seems to indicate that he thought a rose or a rotten mushroom by another name would not be as sweet or as malodorous. Thus, he preserved not only names but also occupations. Wolfe's Ed Battle, owner of a cigar store, was Mr. Seaton A. Barbee, who ran a newsstand and cigar store in Asheville. He changed the Millard Livery Company to Miller and Cashman's Livery Stable, Foster to Forman, *J*ohn Sk*al*ly T*erry* to *Jerry Al*sop, Pickelsimer to Pickleseimer, the Palace Theatre to the Princess Theatre, and Finkelstein to Teitlebaum. Clarence Sawyer's grocery store he called Sawyer's grocery store, and Stikeleather became the simpler Leathergood. In changing Dr. Daniel E. Sevier to Dr. Ned Revere he not only used a rhyme for the surname, but he also reversed the letters of *Dan* to get *Ned.* Vance Street, named for Governor Zebulon Baird Vance, was named Baird Street, for the Governor's middle name. Such changes, if all were known, would be almost endless.

Being an autobiographical writer and having written as completely as possible the story of his early life in *Look Homeward, Angel,* Wolfe was not able to re-create so excellent a work when he again turned to his youth in *The Web and the Rock.* The methods, the subjects, and the form of the section of this book that deals with his life in Asheville prove its comparative inferiority as a whole. There is, in the first place, much overlapping in subject matter and characters, if not in incident. Although the dominant motifs vary from those of the first book, the background is the same. To avoid repeating himself excessively, Wolfe largely gave up descriptions of the members of his immediate family. George Webber lives with Aunt Maw but yearns for his father and his father's world. His Uncle Mark Joyner provides the masculinity of George's life, but at best he makes a most inferior W. O. Gant. For Helen and Luke Gant, and Ben and Little Stevie, those marvelous portraits in *Look Homeward, Angel,* Wolfe substituted descriptions of the

Joyners, who represent his mother's kin. Approximately one-third of the section on the youth of Webber is given to descriptions of his father and the Joyners and to the antagonism of the two worlds that they represent. These passages make up the beginning and the end of this section, and they are interspersed irregularly throughout, apparently with little or no attention to any particular organization or form.

Reveries, childhood superstitions, and the thoughts of George account for the most subjective passages that describe the new hero; and these, also with little apparent scheme, are another important motif of the early section. Webber contrasts the evils of South Carolina with the wonders and goodnesses of Old Catawba, he concocts a system of superstitions and sorceries to suit every occasion and time, he dreams that he follows a circus and visits his father's old home in Pennsylvania, he develops a hatred of mountain grills, and always he dreams of the glorious city. These random thoughts give Wolfe an opportunity to display his lyricism and to try to make Webber a new version of Eugene Gant. A single child, however, living with a puritanical old maid aunt was for Wolfe a much more difficult subject than a child surrounded by brothers, sisters, and boarders. In the new novel Wolfe had limitations imposed because of the necessity of avoiding repetition.

Often in this second writing about a boy in Asheville, Wolfe substituted denunciations of corrupted former mountaineers for the details of narratives, boyhood, and characters that he had treated so thoroughly in his first book. These mark the growth of his social consciousness, while serving as descriptive backgrounds for the future life of Webber. They are much more harsh and unkind to the town as a whole than any of his earlier writings were. Young Eugene had seen romance and wonder even in the slums of "nigger town," but Wolfe had changed his attitudes, and the condemnation of the slums of Libya Hill perhaps reflects maturer thought and greater antagonism. He did not censor and delete his growing dislike of the oppression of the underprivileged. The mountain grills had assumed several new meanings for him, and perhaps the resultant naturalistic condemnations destroy the kind of childhood that Wolfe meant Monk Webber to have. There is maturity, not developing childhood, in the snarl at the manner of man's conception in the slums of Asheville:

> He had been begotten in some casual and forgotten moment . . . , begotten instantly as they were flung back rudely on the edge of an untidy bed. . . . He had been begotten . . . by the idiot, blind hunger of a lust so vile that it knew no loathing for filth, stench, foulness, haggish ugliness, and asked for nothing better than a bag of guts in which to empty out the accumulations of its brutish energies.[1]

Look Homeward, Angel is the better novel for not having social essays of this sort, in which the thought is far too mature for the hero. It makes an essay, but it does not help make a novel.

The details of Altamont are so inseparable from and vital to the life of Eugene Gant that the reader of *Look Homeward, Angel* almost invariably sees their pertinence to the growth and maturity and family of a Southern boy. Eugene is always a vital part of his environment; Monk Webber seems more aloof. He sees as much but participates in less. More than anything else Wolfe wrote, this early section of *The Web and the Rock* is made up of separate sketches, vignettes, and sensational episodes that do not substantially involve the hero, reveal the de-

[1] *The Web and the Rock*, 60–61.

velopment of his character, or advance a single thread of narrative in any direction. What there is of unity springs from an attempt to give through these many vignettes a description of life in a small Southern city. George Webber sees all the actions but is not active in them, or even so lyrically responsive to them as Eugene Gant. Each episode is artistic in itself, but all of them are not given continuity, made relevant to the life of the hero, and welded into a whole. One might perhaps maintain that they do have a unified theme in their being the means of a young man's encountering life in many forms, but this as a total impression is inadequate. Perhaps the weaknesses here may be attributed to the handicaps Wolfe faced when he tried to use his own youth as the basis for a second novel. Placed in the more complete framework of *Look Homeward, Angel,* as perhaps they were in the uncut manuscript that Wolfe submitted on his first book, these tales would then perhaps have a unity that is not revealed in the early life of Webber.

Most of these independent episodes afford excellent opportunities to see how Wolfe took the raw materials of Southern and mountain life and converted them into fiction, and some show him creating in a new and different way. Some of his greatest achievements in short fiction were woven into this early life of Webber. All these supposedly fictitious events are apparently based on actual happenings, but not all of them afford a good opportunity to study Wolfe's creative change and adaptation. The overtones of racial status and conflict and of violence that Wolfe infused into the description of the deadly fight between the Negro Simpson Simms's big dog and the Potterhams' bulldog are probably mostly from Wolfe's keen insight and additions, but it is possible that racial violence almost flared up from a dog fight that he saw as a child. That there can be creative observation is shown in this incident as in many others that Wolfe described. Anyone can see a huge dog leave a fight dripping blood on the sidewalk, but Wolfe's description of the big dog's "dropping big blood flakes on the pavement as he goes" evokes a powerful image because of the several layers of connotation in the word *flakes.*

One can never be positive that any portion of Wolfe's narratives has been invented. Nebraska Crane has been the best example of a character for whom no prototype is known. In his preface to *You Can't Go Home Again,* for example, Edward C. Aswell wrote: "If Tom never wrote anything but naked autobiography, one would have to assume that Nebraska is a counterpart of someone Tom knew as a boy. But not at all. . . . His mother, his sister, Mrs. Ralph Wheaton, and his brother Fred—all have exceptional memories for people who have ever, in even the remotest way, touched their own lives or family. . . . But each of them has told me that there was no one among Tom's childhood acquaintances who could have sat for the portrait of Nebraska." That statement was made several years before the recent publication of *The Letters of Thomas Wolfe.* However, while Wolfe was writing *The Web and the Rock,* in February, 1938, he admitted in a letter to sports writer Arthur Mann that there was a prototype of Nebraska: "I have got the man, I knew him as a child—he never made the Big League, but he could have." Actually, Wolfe used this prototype because of his elemental goodness and simplicity. He wished to create a character that would be "strong, simple, full of earth and sun. . . ."[2]

In creating Nebraska and Nebraska's father, Wolfe was even more interested in the typical than he had been before. He de-

[2] *Letters,* 722–23.

scribes, for example, all the times that Nebraska's father goes to wrestle at the City Auditorium rather than devoting his whole attention to the one most spectacular match he had ever seen: "What nights they were—the nights of smoke-smell, stillness, and the far-off barking of a dog, a fire of oak leaves at the corner, and the leaping fire-dance of the boys around it—great nights of the approaching contest of the wrestlers, the nights of frost and menace, joy and terror—and October!"

Even the one-page description of the wrestling match lacks the dramatic impact of the specific narrative, because it seems to be a composite account of many matches that Monk Webber saw. Yet even these general creations are based very specifically on the life of Asheville as Wolfe had known it. All those "Bone-Crushing Swedes, Horrible Huns, Desperate Dagoes, and Gorilla Gobs," who were, Wolfe says, really retired cowhands, plasterers, bakers, and former house painters, and who wrestled Mr. Crane, were the sort of wrestlers who came to Asheville. Modern wrestling on television has lost all the excitement and glory that once belonged to wrestling in the little mountain town. Wolfe's description is set even before the time when men poured out of the mountains to towns where they could listen to the description of the Dempsey-Tunney fight on the new miraculous wonder, the radio. Judging from the Asheville papers, excitement was even greater in the earlier time. Sports involved a local loyalty that has been lost in the professionalism and cosmopolitanism of most modern athletic contests. Often the papers raised a hullaballoo for days before a local athlete competed with someone from outside the mountains. When western North Carolina's local hero, "Big Tom" Frisbee, fought Professor A. Ono, a Japanese jujitsu expert, in 1905, over two thousand persons attended. "People of all classes are preparing to be present," the *Citizen* announced, "and among them will be Asheville's 'Four Hundred,' for ladies may attend this scientific event with as much propriety as they would an opera. . . ."[3] Big Tom was introduced by former State Senator Murray of Madison County; Professor Ono, by a physician. The unfortunate loss of Big Tom to the Professor was recorded as the headline story on the front page, and the tone of part of the article was elegiac: "There were only two chapters to the tragedy, but 'sufficient unto the night was the sorrow thereof,' as far as Tom was concerned." But the paper was bitter, too. It even quoted the referee, Professor Schoenfeld, a wrestler imported from New Orleans, as saying that Frisbee "has a yellow streak in him."[4] Yet Frisbee and the Professor's match was only one of many that aroused attention. Indeed, Wolfe's account of the wrestling is no more exaggerated and romanticized than were the attitudes of the papers and the people of Asheville.

After two-thirds of this account of the second youth of the Wolfean hero is completed, the manner and subject matter of the novel change. Pages 106 to 157 include a series of character sketches and vignettes of violence, tied together only by George Webber's observation and their presentation of the multifarious forms of life in a small Southern town. One of the most pathetic portraits is that of "Pretty Polly," who has acquired this name because she looks parrot-like and has "a parrot's throaty voice," and who "was a good soul, with fluffy, sandy-reddish hair, a hooked nose, a red face, and teeth that stuck out."[5] When she stops playing during the motion pictures at the Gaiety Theatre,

[3] *Asheville Citizen*, August 2, 1905.
[4] *Ibid.*, August 5, 1905.
[5] *The Web and the Rock*, 113.

the audience cries "Music, Polly, music!" "She never seemed to mind at all, and would play again." Old people in Asheville still remember the character Wolfe described and her playing at Mr. Lynch's theatre on Pack Square. They still recall her thin figure, her hair worn in waterfall fashion, and her prominent teeth.

Other well-remembered local characters make their appearance in this section of *The Web and the Rock*. One is Captain Suggs, whose legs were amputated in the Civil War, and who "was a gigantic hulk, with enormous shoulders, powerful, thick hands, and a look of brutal power and determination about his great, thick neck and his broad, clean-shaven, cruel-lipped mouth."[6] In fiction he is the father of "Fielder" Suggs, former professional baseball player who is making a fortune from the two theaters he owns on the square. There is also Mrs. Charles Montgomery Hopper, who keeps a boardinghouse, but who has bludgeoned her way to social prominence by an imposing name and brazen claims of aristocracy for herself and her boarders.

As Wolfe used well-remembered characters, he also used well-known incidents, of which some can in one way and another be traced back to the facts as they were recorded in the daily papers. Despite some comedy, these are far less humorous and satirical than passages of this sort were in *Look Homeward, Angel*. Wolfe's writing many tragic vignettes with little continuity between them results in a somewhat different interpretation of his hero, the home town, and Southern life. George Webber, in fact, sees more tragedy per page than did Eugene Gant. Rufus Higginson's toy cannon explodes and burns his face horribly. Mrs. Mabel Wheaton recalls at least two incidents of this sort that Wolfe might have had in mind.

[6] *Ibid.*, 111.

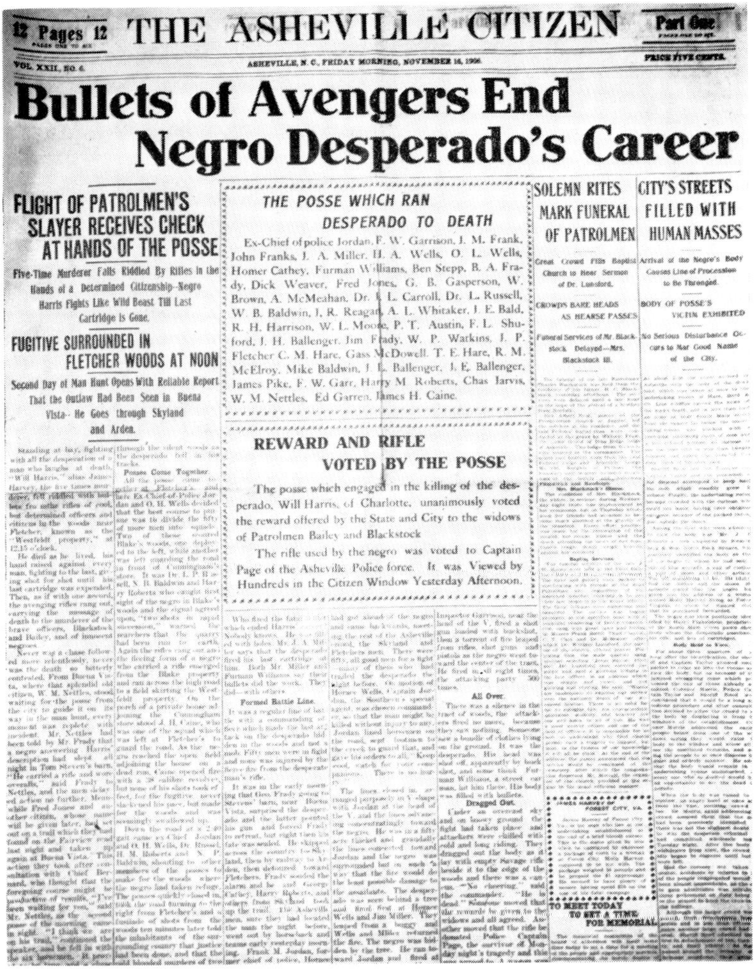

12 Pages 12

THE ASHEVILLE CITIZEN

Part One

VOL. XXII, NO. 6.

ASHEVILLE, N. C., FRIDAY MORNING, NOVEMBER 16, 1906.

PRICE FIVE CENTS.

Bullets of Avengers End Negro Desperado's Career

FLIGHT OF PATROLMEN'S SLAYER RECEIVES CHECK AT HANDS OF THE POSSE

Five-Time Murderer Falls Riddled By Rifles in the Hands of a Determined Citizenship—Negro Harris Fights Like Wild Beast Till Last Cartridge Is Gone.

FUGITIVE SURROUNDED IN FLETCHER WOODS AT NOON

Second Day of Man Hunt Opens With Reliable Report That the Outlaw Had Been Seen in Buena Vista—He Goes through Skyland and Arden.

THE POSSE WHICH RAN DESPERADO TO DEATH

Ex-Chief of police Jordan, F. W. Garrison, J. M. Frank, John Franks, J. A. Miller, H. A. Wells, O. L. Wells, Homer Cathey, Furman Williams, Ben Stepp, B. A. Frady, Dick Weaver, Fred Jones, G. B. Gasperson, W. Brown, A. McMeahan, Dr. L. L. Carroll, Dr. L. Russell, W. B. Baldwin, J. R. Reagan, A. L. Whitaker, J. E. Baldwin, R. H. Harrison, W. L. Moore, P. T. Austin, F. L. Shuford, J. H. Ballenger, Jim Frady, W. P. Watkins, J. P. Fletcher C. M. Hare, Gass McDowell, T. E. Hare, R. M. McElroy, Mike Baldwin, J. L. Ballenger, J. E. Ballenger, James Pike, F. W. Garr, Harry M. Roberts, Chas Jarvis, W. M. Nettles, Ed Garren, James H. Caine.

REWARD AND RIFLE VOTED BY THE POSSE

The posse which engaged in the killing of the desperado, Will Harris, of Charlotte, unanimously voted the reward offered by the State and City to the widows of Patrolmen Bailey and Blackstock

The rifle used by the negro was voted to Captain Page of the Asheville Police force. It was Viewed by Hundreds in the Citizen Window Yesterday Afternoon.

SOLEMN RITES MARK FUNERAL OF PATROLMEN

Great Crowd Fills Baptist Church to Hear Sermon of Dr. Lunsford.

CROWDS BARE HEADS AS HEARSE PASSES

Funeral Services of Mr. Blackstock Delayed—Mrs. Blackstock Ill.

CITY'S STREETS FILLED WITH HUMAN MASSES

Arrival of the Negro's Body Causes Line of Procession to Be Thronged.

BODY OF POSSE'S VICTIM EXHIBITED

No Serious Disturbance Occurs to Mar Good Name of the City.

TO MEET TODAY TO SET A TIME FOR MEMORIAL

Page 1 of the Asheville Citizen *that ran the story about "Will Harris."*

One January night a horse falls, and after Webber hears the two shots that deliver the animal from its misery, "light and warmth went from the boy's life, and the terror of the dark was all about him."

Webber sees a livery stable burn on a winter night, and two incidents stand out in his mind: the insane anguish of Pretty Polly's beau, Duke Mears, when he hears the horses' frantic screaming; and the sight and smell of the dead horses on the morning after the fire. Here Wolfe's memory and selection are interesting because of his omission of some of the most spectacular details. Actually, he might have had in mind either one or both of two fires. When the Millard Livery Company burned in the winter of 1914, five mules and four horses were lost, forty to fifty of them were turned loose in the streets, and the fancy carriages once owned by George W. Vanderbilt were destroyed. When the Chambers and Weaver Company burned in 1915, forty-two horses were lost, one of which was the famous "Old Gray," whose death caused the *Citizen* to give an entire column to the commemoration of the horse and his good qualities. Children loved him because he was the only horse in Asheville to learn to drink from the water fountains provided for human beings. These details belong to the social history of the town, but in the novel they would have been superfluous and perhaps sentimental.

One of the most violent sections of this part of *The Web and the Rock* is that called "The Butcher," in which Wolfe describes the Lampley family. At first, Webber finds "glory and enchantment" in the odors of the rickety machine that Mr. Lampley uses to deliver the meats he sells, but these people become horrible when they introduce the boy to violence and evil. Mr. Lampley is a quiet, scarred man who "never seemed to bat his eyelids" over "his small black eyes," and who has "beyond his family, not one intimate or friendly connection." He has married a huge woman who tells savage stories and screams with laughter as she tells them. She describes her father's cutting open the stomach of a Negro who protests the price of a piece of meat, and she laughs at "the look upon that nigger's face!" She laughs when her son seduces a girl but beats her fifteen-year-old daughter for staying out till ten o'clock "until the blood soaked through her dress an' run down on the floor." When the son steals from his employer and leaves town, Mr. Lampley tells Aunt Maw that he has tried to do right by the boy by beating him "till the blood ran down his back," and that the boy is not coming back, "because if he does . . . I'll kill him. And he knows it."

Thoroughly in keeping with the other descriptions of violence in *The Web and the Rock*, this incident seems to be based on characters known by Wolfe as a child. Research in Asheville, however, revealed no one whom Wolfe might have used until I learned that he imported the Lampleys from outside North Carolina. He met and heard about these people in Pennsylvania, when he visited his father's home. This represents one of the most unusual developments in Wolfe's use of what he knew in life. He was getting geographically farther from his sources, yet at the same time maintaining a unity of tone and the seeming indigenousness of the material.

Two vignettes about automobile accidents create two entirely different moods in *The Web and the Rock*. The first is tragic. Albert and Johnny Andrews coast down a hill in a wagon and run in front of a car. Albert's face is smashed, and his back and legs are broken: "Something immense and merciless that no one understood had fallen from the sky upon him and broken his back and no one could save him now." Johnny has "only two blue sunken marks upon his forehead," but he dies at the scene of the accident. Albert dies two hours after he is taken to the hospital. Mrs. Andrews screams "like a demented hag" when she sees how her real son Albert is injured, but she grows "calm, silent, almost tranquil" when she learns that her adopted child, Johnny, is dead. This contrast of emotions is one of the focal points of this episode, and the other is on George Webber's wonder at the crippled and wasted father and at "the seminal mystery of nature that could draw forth life in swarming hordes from the withered loins of a walking dead man such as this."

In this incident the similarities of Thomas Wolfe and George Webber are so great that no distinction can be drawn. An accident of this sort occurred when Wolfe was in his adolescence. Two children coasted down Vance Street in their toy wagon and had a collision with an automobile at the corner of Woodfin and Vance, very near Tom Wolfe's home. The day, Wolfe said, was "wet to feel," and a reporter wrote that "heavy clouds and a steady rain have kept the little fellows in doors through yesterday." The younger child, a nephew of the people with whom he lived, died forty-five minutes after he reached the hospital, but the son, although seriously hurt, survived. The emotions of the mother, as Wolfe described them, must have seared his soul when he was a child. Like Wolfe, the paper described how one of the boys received multiple injuries on his face, how passers-by took the boys to the hospital, and how several children (probably Tom Wolfe was one of them) saw the accident.

In comic contrast to the tragic accident is the description of another automobile wreck that occurred near the Wolfe home.

Lon Pilcher, some drunken chorus girls, an excited policeman, and fragments of Pilcher's 1910 Cadillac are strewn over fifty yards of pavement, but in this slapstick comedy in both life and fiction nothing but dignity is injured: " 'D'ye think it's damaged much, Mr. Joyner? D'ye think we can fix her up again, so she will run?' Here he belched heavily, covered his mouth with his hand, said 'Excuse me,' and began to prowl drunkenly among the strewn fragments."

Finally in this section one of the best short stories Wolfe ever wrote, and the only one he ever succeeded in publishing in the *Saturday Evening Post*, is woven into the fabric of this life of George Webber—"Child by Tiger." Dick Prosser, the central character of the narrative, is introduced casually as he retrieves a football for Webber and his friends. One of his chief attributes is the respect and humility of the Southern darky—he calls even the boys "Mister." A former soldier, he does every task with meticulousness, even splitting kindling with "a power, a clean precision, a kind of military order." He is, on the one hand, orderly and clean and very religious in all he does, but he is also a near-perfect marksman, a good boxer, and "cunning and crafty as a cat." He shows the boys how to kick and throw a football, how to make a fire, and how to do many things dear to a boy's heart.

Yet from the moment of his appearance in Libya Hill, there is a mysterious enigma in his character. He moves "too softly, at too swift a pace . . . sometimes like a cat." The boys feel "a shadow at their back . . . something moving in the night." If he is religious, he is also an extremist. Time and time again Wolfe uses predominant symbols of darkness and stealthy, catlike movement, images that connote the jungle, the primitiveness of Dick Prosser's race, and the catlike movements of evil.

Despite the goodness of the admired black man, the symbols foreshadow the lurking evil of the seemingly tamed tiger, and they are reinforced by Dick's angry eyes, "shot with red," after he is attacked and beaten by a drunk. The good-natured black wench in the Shepperton's home suddenly becomes as "silent-sullen as midnight pitch" (revealing the contagiousness of Dick's dark evil) and leaves without a credible explanation. When the boys find an army rifle in Dick's room, suddenly he is "on them like a cat . . . like a great, dark shadow before they know it." Dick's sudden change and affable explanation do not entirely dispel their fears.

Even the land and other men reflect the dualism in the Negro. After soft snow covers Libya Hill, Wolfe describes all men and the earth as being divided into good and evil symbols: "In every man there are two hemispheres of light and dark, two worlds discrete, two countries of his soul's adventure. And one of these is the dark land, the other half of his heart's home, the unvisited domain of his father's earth."

These contrasts in character serve as the background for the violence of Dick's character. He has a quarrel with the husband of the Shepperton's maid and kills him with the army rifle that the boys have seen. Then he goes berserk, kills a policeman, and shoots another through the wrist, kills a groceryman who is calling police, shoots an old Negro janitor when he sticks his head out a window, shoots at and misses a drunken judge, critically injures the judge's crony, and drills "squarely through the center of the [telephone] pole, and shot [policeman] John Chapman through the heart." Before the posse finally kills him after he runs out of ammunition on the third day of the chase, he kills a total of seven men. His body is displayed in the window of an undertaker's, and George Webber and his friends see it and try to remember the good of the Negro. They "tried wretchedly to make themselves believe that once this thing had spoken to them gently, had been partner to their confidence, object of their affection and respect. And they were sick with nausea and fear, for something had come into their lives they could not understand."

As the story ends, Wolfe returns to the goodness of the Negro by describing how the boys go into Dick's spotless little room and see his Bible as he had left it open at the Twenty-third Psalm. The room is locked forever, but Dick is not forgotten. Wolfe rounds out the story and completes the imagery of the cat and evil by quoting from Blake's poem "The Tiger," which asks the ageless question about the source of evil:

> *Tiger! Tiger! burning bright*
> *In the forests of the night,*
> *What immortal hand or eye*
> *Could shape* [sic] *thy fearful symmetry?*

This story of the ambiguity of good and evil within one character is perhaps the most interesting single document in the study of Wolfe's imaginative creation and his use of fact. The murders and the mob scene are based directly on the past of Asheville. The parallels to the actual case are minute. Dick Prosser is Wolfe's name for the Negro, Will Harris, but the curious thing about the changes of names is that in fiction Wolfe gave the villain's real name, Harris, to the lover (not a husband, as in the novel) of the Negro girl over whom the violence started. He called the real Negro porter Toney Johnson "the negro porter, Harris." Why he chose in fiction to give the villain's real name to the innocent member of the love triangle can only be speculated upon. Perhaps it was a lapse of memory, perhaps some strange form of ironical whimsy supposed to emphasize the main point of the story, the ambiguity of good and evil. In the novel the porter is the first victim of the murderer, but in real life this man was not killed or injured at all. He ran to police headquarters to report the beginning of the trouble in the basement of a house on Valley Street in the Negro district.

Parts of the account in the newspaper[7] and the story in *The Web and the Rock* can be compared by summarizing the fiction and using real names in parentheses. A young constable, Sam Willis (Charles R. Blackstock), starts into a Negro shack where Prosser (Harris) is hiding after he has killed the porter Harris (Toney Johnson, who escaped). Lieutenant John Grady (Captain John L. Page) stays outside the house, watches the window, and yells for Prosser to come out. The Negro shoots Grady through the arm and kills Willis as he enters the house. Grady runs to telephone for help and is killed, but Page survived. Prosser then escapes and sees an old Negro janitor lean out of a window to see what is happening. Prosser's shot, wrote Wolfe, "tore the top of the old negro's head off"; it passed through the right eye of the real Negro groceryman Ben Allison. Tom Neil, who was shot in the groin by Harris, and George W. Jackson, who had a bullet to cut "through his trousers and underwear without breaking the skin or drawing a drop of blood," were entirely omitted by Wolfe. One terrible statement that Harris made and that would have been entirely in keeping with Wolfe's theme is also unfortunately omitted. Harris, as he shot Neil, hurled words of defiance: "Nobody cares who I am. I am from Hell and don't care who sends me

[7] For all the following details, see the *Asheville Citizen*, November 14–16, 1906.

back." Then Prosser shoots through a telephone pole and kills John Chapman (J. W. Bailey). Chapman is killed by a shot in the heart; Bailey was shot in the mouth.

In life Mr. Harry Finkelstein armed the crowd with fifty guns and revolvers "without thought of possible return of the instruments of death." The avengers then broke into the Asheville Hardware Company for ammunition, but in "Child by Tiger," Uncle Morris Teitlebaum's pawn shop has secure burglar bars for protection, and the mob breaks open the hardware store that belongs to Webber's Uncle Mark. Thus, Wolfe's mob is made more violent; and, although both Mr. Finkelstein and Uncle Morris sold the army rifle to the Negro, the selfish character and the burglar bars of the latter make him much more vivid. In fiction seven men are killed in all, and again this is exaggeration of violence, for in life only two whites and three Negroes were murdered by the insane Harris. Just before Prosser is mutilated by the posse, he kills Doc Lavender and Wayne Foraker, both deputies, but Will Harris fired at Horace Wells and Jim Miller with no success. Again, exaggeration.

Some of the real facts about this case are most interestingly altered by Wolfe for symbolic purposes. Snow fell in Asheville after Harris' crime and before he was captured. "The snow fell thick and fast," wrote the *Asheville Citizen*, "and none noted it." But in Wolfe's version the "white mystery" of the snow covers the "dark land" in a deeply symbolic way, and it falls before Prosser goes berserk; Wolfe uses it to foreshadow and to establish a mood. Will Harris lost one shoe while he was in flight, and Wolfe used this incident; but in doing so, he made a remarkable adaptation to suit the Negro's created meticulousness and precision. Just before Prosser is surrounded by the posse, he reaches a creek and sits down "calmly on the bank, and, as quietly and methodically as if he were seated on his cot in an army barracks, he unlaced his shoes, took them off, placed them together neatly at his side, and then stood up like a soldier, erect, in his bare feet, and faced the mob."

Because of his interest in unity and the character of the Negro, Wolfe omitted a number of significant details about the community and the posse. The fictitious mobs are always active and violent, but the *Citizen* wrote that the city was sober: "There were no threats, far less cursing than usual, the quiet of Sunday almost save for the many determined people on the streets." Asheville was dominated by an "ominous quiet . . . the quiet of a powder magazine," and even the saloons were closed, by order of the mayor. A Negro man who thought he was being robbed and who got out his gun when a posse ordered him to stop was shot. The paper made a plea against lynching but later wrote that it would "save trouble" if he could be "taken dead." The whites thought the Negroes would turn him in if they knew where he was hiding, but posses searched many Negro houses anyway. The Negroes joined in charity drives for the widows of the men Harris had killed, and the *Citizen* reported that there was no racial tension. After Prosser's death, Wolfe became more interested in the actions of the mob. A crowd goes out to meet those bringing in the body, and Randy Shepperton, Monk Webber, and their friends view the riddled body as it is displayed "in the window of the undertaker's place, for every woman, man, and child in town to see." In life a great mob went out to meet the body, which was returned to town and prominently displayed for all to see. Ten at a time filed into the undertaker's; then twenty, and finally thirty in each group made the ghastly trip.

But the dominant interest throughout "Child by Tiger" is

the enigmatic character of Dick Prosser, and the materials Wolfe used are from a multiplicity of local sources. He never knew Will Harris, who had come to Asheville from Charlotte, North Carolina, on the very day when he went berserk. Two years before, he had broken out of prison while he was serving a twenty-year term for burglary and arson. Wolfe gave Dick no criminal record that would have destroyed his goodness. The paper reported that Harris had been in the army and was a "perfect shot," but Wolfe greatly emphasized his military past in order to make him more deadly as well as more meticulous and precise.

Thus, Wolfe used many details from the life of the most dangerous desperado who ever alarmed mountainous Buncombe County, but he altered them to make the character most memorable. His artistic selection, however, is most supremely evident in his using also for this study the character of the most famous and loved Negro who ever lived in Asheville. The Dick Prosser who is loved by Webber and his friends was not Will Harris, whom Wolfe had not known; but he was drawn from the beloved janitor of the Bingham Academy, who was admired for his intelligence, good humor, devotion, meticulousness, and humility. Wolfe's genius is evident in this fusion of the best and the worst Negroes he had ever heard about and the use of Blake's poem to interpret the awe and mystery of the terrible contrast that resulted.

Added to these two characters used in the composite Dick Prosser was a third Negro man in Asheville, the Reverend Robert Parker Rumley, who won a great folk reputation for preaching over and over the same sermon, which he called "De Dry Bones in De Valley."[8] This tempestuous oration was so famous

[8] This sermon has been reprinted in Floyd C. Watkins, " 'De Dry Bones

that Orville Knight Smith transcribed and printed it in Asheville in 1896. Although apparently altered in some places by an inaccurate transcriber, the printed version is an exaggerated variation of the usual primitive, rhythmical, chanting Negro sermon. Such is the background of Prosser's fanaticism and his sermons to George Webber and his friends. Wolfe must have had in mind the stories he had heard about Rumley's sermon when he wrote of Prosser's preaching:

> "O young white fokes," he would begin, moaning gently, "de dry bones in de valley. I tell you, white fokes, de day is comin' when He's comin' on dis earth again to sit in judgment. He'll put de sheep upon de right hand and de goats upon de left—O white fokes, white fokes—de Armageddon day's a-comin', white fokes—an' de dry bones in de valley."[9]

Here again the background provided by Asheville adds much meaning to Wolfe's fiction.

The use of the University of North Carolina as background for Pine Rock College in *The Web and the Rock* also proves again Wolfe's reliance on autobiography. That football game Monk Webber attends between Pine Rock and Monroe and Madison, in which the Old Catawba team defeats its rival for the first time in nine years, is, for example, based on a real game that Tom Wolfe attended when he was a freshman. The University of North Carolina vanquished the University of Virginia in 1916 for the first time in eleven years. The score was seven to nothing (Wolfe wrote six to nothing). North Carolina's touchdown was scored "midway in the third" quarter (just as Wolfe wrote) with a run of fifty-two yards (Wolfe said fifty-

in De Valley,'" *Southern Folklore Quarterly*, Vol. XX, No. 2 (June, 1956), 136–49.

[9] *The Web and the Rock*, 135.

seven). Perhaps he tried to create a college for Monk Webber different from Eugene Gant's, but he did not veer far from what he had actually known.

Whether Wolfe could have created from still smaller fragments of memory and pure imagination is a matter for conjecture. He was making some progress in "Child by Tiger," but even there the incidents are recognizable. Perhaps it is more important to see how fiction surpasses life than to identify details. The total effect of his memory and his alterations is the creation of town life that is unsurpassed in completeness and in lyricism by any imagined town in American literature. *The Web and the Rock*, in itself, is a minor accomplishment in its description of Asheville, but in the long view Libya Hill reinforces and gives breadth to Altamont. Alone, Monk Webber's youth in a Southern town is incomplete and fragmentary. The combined childhood of Eugene Gant and Webber, which represents the childhood of Tom Wolfe, is a great recording and creation. Altamont, Libya Hill, and William Faulkner's Yoknapatawpha in the many books where they appear are artistic creations of life that in scope and quality account for a great part of the wonder of the modern Southern renaissance. To ask Wolfe to create less from fact would have been perhaps to ask him not to write at all. As his works stand, they are not only artistic writings about Southern life but also the very source of Southern social history.

6. Home to Boom Town

THE PHILOSOPHY that George Webber learns in all the years is that you can't go home again, which Tom Wolfe wrote again and again in his last full-length work. That was what Wolfe learned in his years of exile; but despite the threats of bodily harm and the antagonism felt by Ashevillians, it is not physical fear or, indeed, fear of any sort that prevents the going home. He had gone home and had been accepted, and his home town's opposition to its portrayal (or betrayal, as the citizens thought) in the novels was entirely an irrelevant question. There was a place called Asheville for Tom Wolfe or Libya Hill for Monk Webber, but catching a train to the town and the surrounding mountains did not mean return. Man cannot go back, in the first place, because he himself has changed, and even if he were the same, there would be no spiritual home to return to.

Wolfe attempted a timeless theme in his last novel: "I believe that we are lost here in America," he wrote in his credo, "but I believe we shall be found." Being lost, Americans cannot go back, for George Webber is Wolfe's embodiment of his ideas of a universal problem, and the Germans whom he had once so much admired are also lost and cannot go home. Certainly the Northerners whom he knew were more lost than his hero, more lost than the people Wolfe and Webber wished to go home to.

One of the most explicit statements of the problem is made by Wolfe in a conversation with Randy Shepperton: "America went off the track somewhere—back around the time of the Civil War, or pretty soon afterwards. Instead of going ahead and developing along the line in which the country started out, it got shunted off in another direction—and now we look around and see we've gone places we didn't mean to go."[1] America, Wolfe believed, had been shunted off toward the materialism of the roaring twenties, graft, speculation, false ideas about values, and excessive emphasis on false social and economic standards. The result was the great economic stagnation that began in the late twenties and the oppression of the underprivileged, whether an elevator man whose death in *You Can't Go Home Again* is kept from the aristocrats he served or Negroes who are kept in financial bondage by an old evil blind usurer. That all America is thus lost is seen in the omnipresence in the novel of the theme of greed and stupid, uncultured selfishness. Book II is a study of "The World that Jack Built." Specifically *Jack* refers to Mr. Jack, the husband of Webber's mistress, but his money is also suggested in the title. In this section of the novel Webber discovers the stupidity, the crassness, and the corruption of his mistress' world and rejects her because of this environment. Her acquaintances are more irretrievably lost than any characters in the book. One result of America's violation of her old ideals is the suicide that Foxhall Edwards reads about in the newspaper and deliberates on for more than twenty pages, "The unidentified man [who] fell

[1] *You Can't Go Home Again,* 393.

or jumped yesterday from the twelfth floor of the Admiral Francis Drake Hotel. . . ."

But the evils of America and of her new spirit are best seen, by Wolfe at least, in Asheville and Libya Hill. Perhaps George Webber cannot go home again, but at least he tries, and many chapters in the last novel are directly concerned with the whole theme, attempts to return and failure. Ten chapters and approximately 175 pages, besides many brief passages, find Monk Webber visiting Libya Hill, talking to friends from Libya Hill, or thinking about Libya Hill. Again the home town is the point of reference, as much as it was in any of the earlier books, with the possible exception of *Look Homeward, Angel*. In *You Can't Go Home Again* it is central, not only because it is the place of origin, but also because it has imported all the outside world's materialism and corruption. That is why there is no home to go to.

In the fifth chapter of the novel George Webber receives a telegram in which his uncle informs him of the death of Aunt Maw, the spinster who became his guardian after the separation of his parents and the death of his mother. Promptly he leaves the School for Utility Cultures (really New York University) and starts on a trip to the South and Libya Hill. After a summary of the family background of Webber as it was given in *The Web and the Rock* and a description of the people in the Pennsylvania Station, Wolfe boards Pullman K19 for Asheville. Here he encounters Jarvis Riggs, who is talking of land and speculative prices; Mayor Baxter Kennedy, talking of land and prices; Parson Flack, talking of land and prices. He meets Nebraska Crane, the ballplayer, and the only one from Asheville interested in a simple and honest way of life. But the most startling encounter of all is that with Judge Rumford

Bland, one of Wolfe's best characterizations and the most enigmatic man of evil in all the novels. Although the Judge "possessed remarkable gifts," and although there is some sort of code in his "genuinely, unfathomably evil" mind that enables him to judge the evil of others, he lives by lending money to Negroes at the usury of 5 per cent a week. It is this lecherous old man, long blinded from venereal disease, who first asks Webber if he thinks he can go home again. Evil as he is, he still condemns this new age of speculation:

"Oh—" with a deprecating nod— "a little nigger squeezing here and there, a little income out of Niggertown, a few illegal lendings, a comfortable practice in small usury—yet my wants were few, my tastes were very simple. I was always satisfied with, say, a modest five per cent a week. So I am not in the big money, Parson. I remember many things, but I see now I have spent my substance, wasted all my talents in riotous living—while pious Puritans have virtuously betrayed their town and given their whole-souled services to the ruin of their fellow men."[2]

The Judge's accusations of corruption are ironic because of his own sins. He somehow remains a human being despite his corruption, but the evil that grips Libya Hill is made to seem monstrous, inhumane, depersonalized. It belongs to the community and is, therefore, more terrible than any satanic individual.

Arrived in his home town, Webber meets his friends Randy and Margaret Shepperton, and Randy immediately declares that such people as "Skin-'em alive Mack Judson" and "Old Horse-face Barnes" are "drawing lots right now to see which one gets your shirt and which one takes the pants and B.V.D.'s!" After Aunt Maw's funeral, Delia Flood stays in the cemetery to

[2] *Ibid.*, 87.

talk with Margaret and Monk about speculations on land. Chapter VII, called "Boom Town," continues the same theme. The whole population, Wolfe and Webber believe, are "drunk with an intoxication which never made them weary, dead, or sodden, and which never wore off, but which incited them constantly to new efforts of leaping and thrusting exuberance."

Sam Pennock, a boyhood and college friend, offers to split a commission with Webber if he can get his uncle to sell his home on Locust Street. The town sot, Tim Wagner, has become an oracle whose prophesies (always to buy, never to sell) are invariably followed by the local speculators. Randy Shepperton, Webber's reliable friend, is wrecked and fired by his boss, the apparently genial Mr. David Merrit, who is actually as impersonal and vicious as the Federal Weight, Scales, and Computing Company, which he represents. "The City of Lost Men" is a description of Libya Hill's real-estate speculations and of the consequent ruin. The old quiet town of Monk's youth "was changed past recognition, scarred now with hard patches of bright concrete and raw clumps of new construction. It looked like a battlefield, cratered and shell-torn with savage explosions of brick, cement, and harsh new stucco."

Because of Wolfe's not being in Asheville very much during the great boom in 1924 and 1925, and because he wrote much about Webber's reactions to the boom, the extreme sensationalism of the actual boom in Asheville is much more unbelievable than the novel itself. Yet Wolfe's interpretation of this time of speculation is quite accurate, even if it is more conservative. The great change from the expected is perhaps what offends Webber most. He has returned from a great Northern metropolis hoping to find his own "sleepy little mountain village," but the streets that he has remembered for their "early-afternoon emptiness and drowsy lethargy, were now foaming with life, crowded with expensive traffic, filled with new faces he had never seen before." Yet this interpretation is a mere echo of statements made many times before in Asheville with condemnation or complacency. Smugly the *Asheville Times* wrote in July, 1924, of Haywood Street: "There is an air on the street of activity; it hasn't been so long since the atmosphere was suggestive of easy-going laziness."[3]

A good-will tour made by many Ashevillians to Florida in the spring of 1925 helped to begin the tragedy by making the Florida speculators aware of the virgin opportunities for exploitation in the mountain resorts of western North Carolina.[4] When the Florida boom began to slump, these profiteers left the underwater lots they had sold and came north to Asheville. Their activities in the mountain town were so spectacular that Wolfe wisely chose not to use the most lurid details, because they would have seemed so improbable in fiction. From Florida they brought with them their "party girls" and "cold eyed babes," as Clarence R. Sumner recently described them in the *Citizen,* "trained in brittle small talk and capable of wheedling Grandpa out of his false teeth and making him like it."[5] For the foolish widows and dowagers who needed some sweet wheedling before investment, the real-estate men also had "party boys."

Many swindlers and big-time operators rented the first floors of the best buildings on the best streets, removed the old fronts, installed folding doors and hardwood floors, and brought in potted palms and orchestras. Even the most riotous accounts

[3] *Asheville Times,* July 27, 1924.
[4] *Asheville Citizen,* August 29, 1935.
[5] *Ibid.,* March 16, 1952.

of the manners of the roaring twenties in Hollywood and New York do not surpass life in Asheville. Aware of the necessity of appearances and geniality, salesmen wore tweeds or golf socks and knickers. The *Citizen* in 1926 reported that real estate had replaced barrooms as the leading business of the city.[6] They chartered buses to carry out-of-towners to prospective development areas, where "orchestras and bands tooted away in secluded coves and pastures in the environs of the city, and customers were fed watermelon and lemonade and other beverages perhaps more to their liking."[7] Expenditures on advertising were as unbridled as the wild emotions of the speculators. There were, for example, great auction sales featuring loud music and barbecue. Every issue of the daily papers was filled with news, editorials, and feature articles about development projects. Salesmen with megaphones shouted the virtues of their lots from street corners and on the lots themselves.[8]

God had not built the mountains to suit all the fancies of the real-estate speculators, who spared no expense and trouble in changing the geography of Asheville. "They had torn down ancient buildings," Wolfe wrote, "and erected new ones large enough to take care of a city of half a million people. They had leveled hills and bored through mountains, making magnificent tunnels paved with double roadways and glittering with shining tiles—tunnels which leaped out on the other side into Arcadian wilderness." Artificial lakes were built, and whole mountains were leveled.[9] Fantastic, overly poetic names were given to suburban areas: Country Club Estates, Panther Mountain Estates, Mountain Meadows Estates, Stradley Mountain

6 *Ibid.*, November 21, 1926.
7 *Ibid.*, March 16, 1952.
8 Raleigh *News and Observer*, March 21, 1937.
9 *Ibid.*

Park, Sulphur Springs Park, Wild Acres, Royal Pines, Hollywood-in-the-Hills, and many others.[10] Without using exactly the same names, Wolfe satirized this poetic nomenclature; he used "Wild Boulders," "Shady Acres," and "Eagle's Crest."

The American's love for the "bigger and better," for size for its own sake, and for numbers as the chief means of measurement is typical of Asheville and Libya Hill. Again and again Wolfe quotes the conversations on increases in prices and profits from speculation. In fiction and in reality the town went mad over unrealized paper profits. The site of the George W. Vanderbilt Hotel on Haywood Street was appraised in 1920 and 1921 for $150 a front foot, but in 1924 it was worth over $3,000 a front foot, an increase of 2,000 per cent in three years. In 1894, a lot on the same street sold for $15,000, but thirty years later E. W. Grove paid $100,000 for fifty feet of the same property. Had all of this land been sold at the same rate, it would have brought $700,000, an increase of 4,626 per cent in thirty years. Another lot jumped from $16,000 to $250,000 in ten years.[11] In 1925, the register of deeds in Buncombe County had to enlarge his office and employ more personnel.[12] The same paper that announced this expansion also described how some Floridians had bought three thousand acres near Asheville for $1,000,000 and were starting a vast new real-estate project. Numerous other examples might be cited. The paper profits of $50,000 made by Webber's friend Sam Pennock in two hours and of $300,000 in two months are not much more fantastic than what actually happened.

One of the most fantastic careers in all of Asheville's history

[10] *Asheville Citizen,* August 29, 1935.
[11] *Asheville Times,* July 27, 1924.
[12] *Asheville Citizen,* September 9, 1925.

became even more incredible because of the real-estate speculation. Wolfe had an extraordinary source for the character J. Timothy Wagner, who wastes two fortunes before he is twenty-five and then becomes "preëminently the town sot." For a time Tim makes his home in a horse-drawn hearse, which has been given to him by an undertaking firm that has bought motor-driven vehicles. Once some loafers in McCormack's drug store see him occasionally "swallow something and then shudder convulsively." After several repetitions of this action, they discover that each time he is catching a goldfish and swallowing "a wriggling little shape," long before such wild adventures became characteristic of the twenties. The life of J. Timothy Wagner acquires a new grandeur during the great boom in Libya Hill. "Diseased and broken," "addled now with alcohol," he becomes the local real-estate divining rod. Now he owns a magnificent automobile, "a glitter of nickel, glass, and burnished steel." He carries a Malacca cane, wears "lemon-colored gloves," and has a chauffeur—all these probably financed by donations from the real-estate adventurers whom he has told to buy, never to sell.

Here Wolfe was using his old methods. Just as Asheville had provided picturesque characters for his description in *Look Homeward, Angel* of life in a small town, Asheville again provided the characters for his use in the description of the catastrophic change. The prototype of this character has been described in an article in the *Citizen*. "Heelers," the reporter says, were "hanging on every word he uttered, ready to run, not walk to the nearest real estate office and get their binder money on the barrel head."[13] The goldfish incident was true. This local character "paralyzed an audience in a downtown drug store by

[13] *Ibid.*, March 16, 1952.

reaching into an aquarium and calmly munching a couple of the finny beauties."[14] For a time he did live "in an abandoned hearse parked on a lot just off Church Street." Had Wolfe needed them, the life of the real Tim could have provided other sensational details. He was a member of a pioneer family. Although the reporter did not, as Wolfe did, comment on his wasting two fortunes, probably elements of that story are true. Tim was also a yarn spinner, and he could mimic hogs so well that he was accused of being able to converse with them, but he denied it.

Book III of *You Can't Go Home Again* begins with a figurative comparison of America in 1929 with a cicada: "It had come to an end and a beginning." "The leaders of the nation," wrote Wolfe, "had fixed their gaze so long upon the illusion of a false prosperity that they had forgotten what America looked like." Asheville, then, merely provided one of the most bizarre examples of what Wolfe wished to write about. Again he was fortunate in his origins, for the bursting of the Asheville bubble was as sensational as any deflation in the country, and it was a perfect illustration of Wolfe's new economic interpretation of America.

When Asheville made its compulsory, abrupt, and violent return to sanity and depression, every real-estate company but one failed.[15] One strange thing was that the sinking ship carried with it many rats who had clambered aboard only at the last moment. After the decline started, men who had remained aloof and refused to buy rushed in with their money where even the speculators themselves refused to tread. For a time the newcomers created the false impression that a new boom was

[14] *Ibid.*, August 22, 1948.
[15] *Ibid.*, August 29, 1935.

on, but finally they too lost all they had. At nine o'clock on a "Black Thursday" in November, 1930, four banks failed to open their doors, and the resulting trials of more than a score of bankers and politicians dragged on for months. The development of residential, public, and business properties proved futile. School and business buildings remained unused and vacant; weeds grew up and covered some of the real-estate developments; indeed, in some of the houses the electric current was never turned on. As early as 1927 Asheville had eighteen hundred vacant houses.[16] The Fleetwood Hotel on Jumpoff Mountain, near Hendersonville, North Carolina, remained an unfinished thirteen-story skeleton. This intended resort for the wealthy represented an investment of one and a half million dollars, but it served only two minor and ridiculous purposes: people were charged ten cents admission to see the unfinished ruin; and when it was about ten years old, it was torn down so that its steel might be put into bridges.[17]

George Webber in New York on March 12, 1930, opens the *New York Times* and finds an account of the failure of the Citizens Trust Company in Libya Hill. Actually, the Central Bank and Trust Company, which provided the source in this instance, failed in November of that year, and Wolfe read about it in a London paper.[18] Webber reads also of the "rather mysterious death . . . with a bullet through his head," of Mayor Baxter Kennedy, one of the land-mad and money-crazy travelers whom Webber met on the train when he last visited Libya Hill. Events described in the newspaper cause Webber to recall the past and such people as the Mayor and Jarvis Riggs, who,

16 Raleigh *News and Observer*, March 21, 1937.
17 *Asheville Times*, April 15, 1937.
18 *Letters to His Mother*, 203.

despite his respectable and poor origins, had become the cashier of the Citizens Trust Company when it was founded in 1912. (Actually, the Central Bank was founded on March 18, 1912.) Conspiracy between politicians, bankers, and businessmen created "The Ring," "a vast and complex web that wove through the entire social structure of the town," a web of "frenzied finance and speculation and special favors." Two years before the bank failed, the Mayor went to Jarvis Riggs and threatened to withdraw the city's funds. Riggs, however, managed to keep the money by telling the Mayor that withdrawal would mean the ruin of the bank and the town.

Just before noon on the day when the bank fails, Mayor Kennedy is found dead by that evil old blind man, Judge Rumford Bland. As the Judge enters a stinking rest room, his foot touches something in the dark, and as he feels to see what the object is, he plunges his fingers "into the foundering mass of what just five minutes before had been the face and brains of a living man." Almost every detail in this climactic part of *You Can't Go Home Again* is based on happenings in Asheville. A mayor of the town killed himself in a rest room on the fourth floor of one of the business buildings. His suicide came soon after he was indicted; Wolfe just intensified the drama by having the event occur on the day of the failure of the bank. A blind attorney heard the shot. Judge Bland more dramatically hears no shot and thus comes upon the body as a total surprise. In reality, he "felt his way into the hallway," the *Asheville Times* reported, "and remained there about three minutes."[19] He and the janitor found the body "slumped over in one corner of the lavatory, which was hardly large enough to accommodate the large body of the former Asheville mayor."

[19] *Asheville Times.*

Wolfe used even the same manner of killing; the real mayor's face was so distorted that identification was extremely difficult. The bullet entered the right temple and came out close to the left ear.

Although Wolfe based the discovery of the Mayor's suicide in his book on the real incident, he did not base Judge Bland's character on that of the lawyer. There are the parallels of profession, blindness, and the discovery of the body. But the real lawyer was a young man who could not have had a past like that which Wolfe created for his character.

For the sake of impact and brevity Wolfe has the Mayor's suicide to come while the crowd is milling around the closed banks. This closeness of events and Wolfe's statement that "six million dollars of public money" was lost made unnecessary any description of charges against Baxter Kennedy. The actual mayor faced "charges of conspiring to pervert the credit of the city and the county, to misapply public funds, and to use public funds for the benefit of a private corporation, the Central Bank and Trust Company."[20] Fiction simplified the moral issues also. The Mayor in *You Can't Go Home Again* is guilty by default of suicide without a note. The real mayor, on the other hand, vehemently declared his innocence and his expectations of acquittal when he was indicted. In his suicide letter "To the People of Asheville," he declared that he and the men in the bank had done no wrong. The last paragraph of the letter was a question: "What would you have done? Would you have closed the bank and lost it, or would you have made an honest effort to save it?"

Twenty-seven men in all were indicted, including Colonel Luke Lea, the tycoon from Tennessee, who, interestingly

[20] *Ibid.*

enough, served as a model for the villain of Robert Penn Warren's *At Heaven's Gate.*[21] Instead of the $6,000,000 in public money that was involved, according to Wolfe's narrative, Asheville and Buncombe County had nearly $9,000,000 in the five banks.[22] Of $10,105,381.41 in all the banks, only $250,000 was at first expected to be refunded.[23] A much larger sum, however, was after many years finally realized by depositors. Of the twenty-seven indicted, a local paper reported in June, 1931, only thirteen defendants were tried, and twelve of these were freed. Only one was convicted, and only one count of more than seventy-five against him was sustained.[24]

The suicide of Baxter Kennedy is the focal or turning point in Wolfe's economic study of the boom in Asheville and America. Actually, it is as typical of the small waves of suicides in Asheville as that of the unidentified man who jumps from the twelfth floor of the Admiral Francis Drake Hotel in Brooklyn is typical in the novel about the numerous suicides in America in 1929. "Forty people," Wolfe greatly exaggerated, "shot themselves within ten days, and others did so later."

All the materials that Wolfe needed in this novel of economic change and evil were immediately available in his home town. If Asheville had once represented the drama and the vitality of life in a small town, she could also represent the corruption of that way of life. This time Wolfe did not even need to exaggerate. His major achievement was the use of the old Judge as a commentator on the great and impersonal evil. Otherwise, the story in *You Can't Go Home Again* is true to life, except for compression, a few minor changes, and Wolfe's

21 *Asheville Citizen,* April 22, 1931.
22 *Asheville Citizen-Times,* February 22, 1931.
23 *Asheville Citizen,* October 23, 1931.
24 *Ibid.,* June 2, 1931.

lyrical and subjective point of view. Here one of the most interesting points, furthermore, is not so much his literal use of his home town as his giving it a larger, national, and universal framework. Monk Webber observes in Libya Hill the same processes that he has seen in New York and the North, places that were expected to fall victim to the evils of speculation. Wolfe believed that in the story of Libya Hill he had told "what happened not only in Asheville but everywhere throughout the country during those years of frenzied gambling and speculation."[25]

The use of Asheville in this way is even more significant because of Wolfe's absence and alienation from the town. He had sensed the decline in the great local boom following 1924, and he had written caustically to his mother about being "born some 23 years ago in a community which bought and sold real-estate."[26] He had attacked the obsession for civic clubs, money, high society, and progress.[27] He had been able to see Asheville during the boom, but in dealing with the bank scandals, he could not work from childhood memory or from what he had observed during short visits. He apparently did not wish to rely on the facts about the Depression in other places, and he had not been in Asheville to observe at first hand. These being the circumstances, Wolfe had to do research. During the trials of the bankers he read all he could find printed in New York and asked his mother to write him what she knew and to save the clippings. He wrote her that he believed one of the accused to be "guilty as hell, but I think we shall live to see the day when he returns and becomes an honored pillar of the Methodist Church again."[28]

[25] *Letters to His Mother*, 285.
[26] *Ibid.*, 71.
[27] *Ibid.*, 76.
[28] *Ibid.*, 206.

His letters all through the Depression show a growing interest in booms and failures and in man's inclination to victimize himself and others economically. Contempt, pity, and regret for the loss "of the old simple unpretending spirit of people" mingle in his attitude toward his home town.[29] Sometimes he used a sympathetic tone in telling his mother of his "sincere regret and sympathy for the misfortune and loss."[30] On February 14, 1938, in the very year of Wolfe's death, while he was still trying to get complete information on the bank scandals, he asked his friend and former teacher, Mrs. Roberts, to send him as much information as she could get.[31] In April, he asked his mother to help him get material on the boom and the period afterward. Mrs. Roberts and a distant relative had promised to help him but had not done so.[32] Later he wrote that his efforts to get a small labor paper, the *Asheville Advocate*, had been to no avail.[33] The *Citizen* and the *Times*, he had heard, were "very evasive and sketchy" in their treatments of the bank scandals. He had had trouble getting what he wanted: "a record of what was public news and that everybody in town knew about."[34] Since this was his last long letter to his mother, apparently he never got what he wanted. More years added to his life might have seen great changes and many more details in his story of boom town that now appears in *You Can't Go Home Again*. As close as Wolfe's story is to life in Asheville, he still wanted it more accurate and exact. How much the further revisions and additions would have improved the

29 *Ibid.*, 260.

30 *Ibid.*, 285.

31 Wolfe, "Writing Is My Life," *Atlantic Monthly*, Vol. CLXXIX, No. 2 (February, 1947), 57.

32 *Letters to His Mother*, 350.

33 *Ibid.*, 353.

34 *Ibid.*

art of the novel is entirely a matter of speculation, but with his changes it might have been a much better book than it actually became.

Abundant evidence proves that great sections of the later books had once been written about Eugene Gant. "Boom Town" was originally published in the *American Mercury* in 1934 as a story about Asheville and many of the Gants who had appeared in the early books. That this short story had once been a part of the manuscript of *Of Time and the River* was indicated in one of Wolfe's letters to his mother.[35] When it was actually first published in the *Mercury*, the characters were all Gants with changed names. Thus, "Boom Town" can serve as a rather typical document in the illustration of Wolfe's changing Altamont to Libya Hill.

Virtually all of the short story was used in *You Can't Go Home Again*, but there were a few omissions, numerous additions, and much reorganization to make it fit not only the life of George Webber but also the over-all pattern of the complete work of which it became a part. "Boom Town" as it first appeared was an imaginary account of the return of the prodigal author, although Wolfe had not been home since the publication of *Look Homeward, Angel* and the bank failures. The return in the short story is merely Eugene's trip home to visit his family, but Monk goes back because of the death of his guardian, Aunt Maw. The journey on the train was briefly described in the story, but in the novel the meetings with Nebraska Crane and all the speculators from home give it much greater length.

John, the name for Eugene in the *Mercury* version, is met at the train station by his mother Delia and his brother Lee, obvi-

[35] *Ibid.*, 285.

ously names that he originally intended to make Eliza and Luke in the novel. With very few changes in characterization in *You Can't Go Home Again,* he simply converted Delia Hawke, who was to have been Eliza Gant, into Margaret Shepperton and Lee into Randy. He changed a few characteristic gestures, took out some of Lee's "Whah-whah-h's!" and that was all. Wolfe was not able to transfer his mother's or Delia Hawke's interest in real estate to Margaret Shepperton; so he created for this purpose a woman named Delia Flood, retaining the first name he had used in the short story. Ironically, when Mrs. Flood goes to Aunt Maw's funeral, it is just as if Mrs. Wolfe were attending her own funeral. In the short story Delia and John drive up to the family graveyard and see the monuments. W. O. Gant has become William Oliver Hawke, "Born near Gettysburg, Pennsylvania, April 16, 1851—Died Altamont, Old Catawba, June 21, 1922." These dates coincide and contrast strangely with those of Mr. Wolfe: April 10, 1851—June 20, 1922. The twins Grover and Ben Wolfe (or Gant) are in the short story Arthur McFarlane Hawke and Edward Madison Hawke. In the novel the lot is the same, but Joyners, the fictitious representations of Mrs. Wolfe's family, are buried there.

Family history becomes intricately involved in the novel. John Webber buries his wife Amelia in the lot of his own choice even though they were separated when she died, but Mark Joyner moves her because "he wouldn't let a sister of his lie in Webber earth." Mr. Hawke in "Boom Town" moves his first wife from one cemetery to another, but no reason is given, except that he just set his mind to move her. Mr. Wolfe twice moved the body of the second of his three wives, one time because of a dispute about the ownership of a lot, and another when he bought the lot where Tom Wolfe and other members of the family are buried in Riverside Cemetery. Different persons look into the coffin in the three accounts (two by Wolfe and one by his mother in *The Marble Man's Wife*). But the growth of Cynthia's (or Amelia's or Lydia's) red hair is noticed in all three. The same Negro man, Prov in the short story and *The Marble Man's Wife,* and Prove in *You Can't Go Home Again,* does the work in every instance. The alterations from short story to novel had to be made because of the change in the hero and the hero's family. The variations from life in the two accounts seem to exist for simplification and thus for greater impact rather than for concealment. Some of the changes involving the family cause great improvements in the novel. Seeing the graves of her deceased twins, Mrs. Hawke in "Boom Town" expresses her hopes for the hereafter: "I believe I'll meet them in a Higher Sphere, along with all the members of our family—all happy and all leading a new life." But this same wish, expressed in the novel by Delia Flood, is applicable to the estranged John and Amelia Webber: "I believe I'll meet them some day in a Higher Sphere, along with all my other friends—all happy, and all leading a new life."

The growth of Wolfe's economic thought in the last years of his life is well illustrated by the chapter on the Federal Weight, Scales, and Computing Company, the Babbit-like executive David Merrit, and the ruthless methods of controlling sales and the salesmen. "You deliver or you go right out on your can! See?" the genial Merrit tells Randy. "The Company doesn't give a damn about you! It's after the business! You've been around a long time, but you don't mean a damn bit more to the Company than anybody else! And you know what's happened to a lot of other guys who got to feeling they were too big for their job—don't you?"

Earlier, in *Look Homeward, Angel,* before the Depression hit and before Wolfe was interested in the theme he developed in *You Can't Go Home Again,* he had written of Hugh Barton simply that the "Federal Cash Register Company, touched by his devotion to duty, rewarded him with a good salary." The biographical background of Barton-Shepperton was provided by the cruel treatment of Wolfe's own brother-in-law. Within the family he found an instance to portray the greed and ruthlessness that he had at last seen in American boom-time speculation and big business.

Some difference in Wolfe's attitude toward local personalities may be noted in the changes made in the character of J. Timothy Wagner when Wolfe included the short story in his novel. J. Rufus Mears, the same person in "Boom Town," serves a term in jail for operating gambling machines and another on the chain gang for bootlegging. An addict to cocaine, he tours small towns with a burlesque show and telegraphs the morning paper a lurid account of his own death by violence. In the novel his career is much tamer. He wastes two fortunes, becomes a sot, swallows goldfish alive, and sleeps in a hearse. The character in the novel is much more comic and fuller developed but less desperate, scandalous, and dangerous. Wolfe seemed to have more pity in this rewriting, to be more compassionate and sympathetic in his last years.

At the very end of the novel George Webber interprets his own life and arrives at a philosophy which is far from any systematic or formal statement of belief but which is also a statement of confidence in the future of America. Writing to Maxwell Perkins, the fictitious Foxhall Edwards, he describes how the people of Old Catawba have tried to explain the bitterness of his first book in terms of a tragedy that happened to him in college. Monk Webber and four other students blindfolded a freshman and forced him to dance on a barrel. The student fell, cut his jugular vein on a broken bottle, and died while trying to smile and show that there was no evil but stupidity in the hazing. Randy Shepperton, three other boys, and Monk Webber "were expelled, brought up for trial, released in the custody of our parents or nearest relatives, and deprived of the rights of citizenship by legislative act."

This incident in *Look Homeward, Angel* would have been an almost literal transcription of life. In *You Can't Go Home Again* it is still based on fact, but Tom Wolfe was never involved. A freshman at the University of North Carolina was killed in a hazing incident several years before Wolfe ever went to the university. The *Asheville Citizen* ran an item about the steps taken to outlaw hazing, and the details given in that article were very similar to the incident as Wolfe described it more than twenty-five years later: "Four students who were forcing . . . [the freshman] to dance on a barrel when he fell and cut his throat on a broken bottle, today were expelled."[36] Mr. J. M. Roberts, Wolfe's teacher in the Old North State Fitting School, said in the year of his death that this incident was based on a talk that he had made to Wolfe's class. Wolfe remembered this speech and used it in his very last novel. All the details come from a combination of imagination and memories of the university and Mr. Roberts' talk. "Plato Grant, our Old Man, our own Philosopher," merely says, "My God, boys, what have you done?" Wolfe knew Professor Horace Williams well,

[36] *Asheville Citizen*, September 27, 1912.

whom he called Plato Grant in fiction, and his reactions as well as the boy's dying smile and Webber's involvement are entirely fictitious.

This incident is but one that shows a change in the genius of Wolfe. There are less lyricism, a greater variation from fact in some instances, a continued use of the family, and, especially, a growing interest in economics, politics, and sociology. There is development, but compared with what the novel would have been if Wolfe had seen it through the press, the change may be embryonic. The theme, that you can't go home, is spiritual rather than geographical. There is no regression to the age beyond profit, speculation, and progress. Wolfe came home again for his subject matter, and Asheville obligingly provided the very evils that kept him and America from returning. Had he lived, Asheville, Altamont, and Libya Hill would have continued to be the focal points of all his fiction. Perhaps there was no return, but there was no escape either. He wished to know more about Asheville and was writing for more information shortly before his death. The tragedy of his death was that his biography and interpretation of American life as he knew it in this Southern town was not complete, and he knew it more than any of his critics.

7. *The Country People of Old Catawba*

THE TRIP TO BURNSVILLE and mountainous Yancey County that Wolfe made on his way home to Asheville in 1937 symbolized his developing interest in his forebears and the history of his native state. "Some deep, unreasoning urge" caused him to put off the moment of return and to visit his mother's kin. Burnsville is still a little town only partially modernized by the aggression of the civilizing tourists and the new ideas of progress that Wolfe so greatly detested. There the blood of the mountaineer has run pure in the racial descent from his ancestors, at times cold like the imperturbable countenance of the American frontiersman, and again hot with the passion of the old Anglo-Saxon—as Wolfe quickly discovered.

"The night had the chill cool of mountain May" as Tom Wolfe and one of his kinsmen walked down the village street and straight into gunfire between two feuding clansmen. "Now, Dock," (I am using fictitious names) Wolfe heard someone say, "you are going too far. Leave me alone." There was, according to newspaper accounts, a quick and futile attempt to separate the two, but Dock pulled his pistol. Wolfe dodged behind a car and heard three or four pistol shots and air escaping from a punctured tire. Then he heard Ed tell Dock, "Go ahead and shoot. I'm not afraid of you."[1] Somehow these two men were separated without any injury, and Wolfe was introduced to Dock as a descendant of native stock.

"So you're the one who had all the trouble with them books," Dock reportedly said. "Well, I'll tell you one thing—you'd better never put me in a God-damn book."[2] Just a little different from the greetings extended over the teacups by his friends in New York.

This episode occurred on a Saturday, and Wolfe went on to Asheville. The next Saturday, Dock and Ed met again, although Wolfe was not present. "Have you got your gun with you?" Ed casually drawled.

"I have."

Roy, a friend of Dock's, made a suspicious move, and Ed warned him not to get behind him. Then Ed returned to Dock, "You haven't got the drop on me you had last Saturday night."

"I have got the difference and I'm going to use it."

An effort to separate them failed, and Ed offered to end the feud, "Take your hands off your gun. Shake hands and be friends."

But Dock said no, shook off the peacemaker, and shot at Ed as he dodged behind a building. Evading a man who was trying to hold him, Ed came back and shot at Dock, but his gun snapped as Dock fired and missed. When Ed stepped from behind the building a second time, both fired and Ed was killed.

Wolfe was in Asheville when Ed was killed, but he heard about it on Sunday morning. His sister says that Tom was driven nearly frantic. He was afraid that Dock had killed Ed not only because of the long-standing hatred but also because

[1] *Asheville Citizen.*
[2] From a conversation with Mrs. Mabel Wheaton.

he wanted to be used as a character in one of Wolfe's books. He was.

In August, Wolfe was a witness in the trial of Dock and Roy. Although Wolfe had not seen the killing, the prosecuting attorney asked him to describe the gun battle that he had seen one week before the killing. Wolfe's testimony was one chief topic of the defense attorney's speech to the jury at the end of the trial. The statements of a creative writer like Wolfe, the shrewd lawyer argued, could not be considered reliable in a court. His fertile imagination was so accustomed to writing fiction that he could no longer distinguish between reality and events conceived in his own mind. Fantastic as this contention sounds, the lawyer was perhaps extremely close to the truth. Dock was sentenced to twelve years and Roy to seven.

"The Return of the Prodigal," in *The Hills Beyond*, tells the story of Ted Reed's killing Emmet Rogers in the county seat of Zebulon, and almost every detail is taken from the episode in Burnsville. The most significant change is that Eugene Gant witnesses the actual slaying, not just the preliminaries seen by Thomas Wolfe. Violence by hearsay would be ineffective in fiction. There is also a change in manner from all Wolfe's earlier stories. The account here is almost as bare and stark as it would have been if Hemingway had written it. Every movement is casual; a good part is told in dialogue, saturated with the understatement of mountain men. The spoken words are "drawling, mountain-quiet, somehow ominous." The beginning of the fatal gun battle, one of the men says, is "a little argument, I guess." Only Ted Reed has a gun in Wolfe's account, and Emmet Rogers, a much braver and more innocent man than the real-life Ed, faces him without a gun and tells him as he shoots that he is not afraid:

A fourth shot—
"Go on! Go on! Goddam you, I'm not—"
A fifth—and silence.

Then Ted sees Eugene and asks who he is:

"Must be a cousin of yours, Ted. Leastways, he's a cousin of mine. You know—the feller who wrote that book."

With a slow and sullen grin Ted shifts the gun and offers his hand. The hand of murder is thick flesh, strong, a little sticky, cool and moist.

"Why, sure, I know about you. I know your folks. But, by God, you'd better never put *this* in a book! Because if you do—"[3]

Thus, Wolfe recorded the event as he knew it, turning again to life and the facts as he always had done before. He ignored the warning, even wrote the warning in his own story. This time, however, there is a wholly new element in his craft—restraint. His description of "the hand of murder" is horrible because it is so simple, primeval, and noncommittal. No flood of the rhetoric of *Look Homeward, Angel* could have made killing so nauseous and awesome, nor could the lyricism have been as appropriate a vehicle for the content. Wolfe was learning to describe mountain men in the simple terms of their own lives and speech.

The Hills Beyond thus presents Wolfe's career in a new phase, which is revealed in this story of the desperate violence he witnessed on his return to the South, in several other stories of this collection, and especially in the fragment that provided the title for the book. All these reveal a desire to record the mores and the history of North Carolina and especially of the

[3] Thomas Wolfe, *The Hills Beyond* (New York, Harper and Brothers, 1941), 129.

people in the mountains. Some of the stories in this volume were written a good while before Wolfe's death; some were finished in the last year of his life; and some were not finished at all. Significantly, *The Hills Beyond* deals with Asheville and the surrounding mountains more in proportion than any book since *Look Homeward, Angel,* which was devoted exclusively to life in North Carolina. The last action in the tenth chapter of the fragmentary novel was dated by Wolfe as approximately 1887, and he had spent all the first part in writing a creative history of his region. In subject matter he was returning home.

In addition to the novel there are ten stories or essays and plays in this last volume. Of these, six are about the South or Asheville or Wolfe's kinsmen. The other four fall mainly into the genre of the essay, and most deal with universal topics rather than with specific episodes from Wolfe's life in the North. All the stories about the South fill in previously unused aspects of the lives of his kinsmen. "The Lost Boy" is an account of the life and early death of Grover Gant. The strange but medically normal physical structure of Eugene Gant is the subject of "No Cure for It," a short story that was once intended to be a portion of *Look Homeward, Angel.* The play *Gentlemen of the Press* is set in a newspaper office in Asheville in 1916. "Chickamauga," one of the best narratives Wolfe ever wrote, is a story of the Civil War as described by Uncle John Westall in his ninety-fifth year. "The Return of the Prodigal" deals with the imaginary and then the real home-coming of Eugene Gant.

Written at different periods in Wolfe's development as a writer, the short selections in *The Hills Beyond* fall into both the Gant and the Webber cycles. Although Eugene is the hero of most of them, many characters from the older books stage reappearances, and characters from both cycles are often used together in the same story. Here is evidence that the break in the narrative when Wolfe buried Eugene and created George Webber was far from sharp and clean-cut. Wolfe was careless in the change, and often he used details that were clearly based upon the books he had written under the guidance of Maxwell Perkins. Had he lived to write more narratives, the Gant and Webber cycles would probably have come closer and closer together, and finally they would perhaps have been inextricably mingled. That disunity and disintegration in all his works that came as a result of the change from Gant to Webber might have gradually disappeared as he used more and more Gant characters in his stories about Webber. Even some of Wolfe's defenders have said that he wrote only one book. Probably he would not have been able to develop an entirely different subject even if he had had the opportunity to write several more long works. His materials were indeed inexhaustible, but his use of biography would have made a unity of all he wrote. Things were so closely related in his mind that he could not dissociate them and begin an entirely different work.

If one may judge from the list of characters in "The Lost Boy," this story was written before Wolfe even thought of Monk Webber and Libya Hill. There is no name of any person that belongs to the Webber cycle. Edward Aswell's statement, however, that it was "written early in 1937" indicates, if it is entirely accurate, that Wolfe deliberately turned back to the Gant books and to a story that he had treated briefly in his first novel.[4] Many characters from *Look Homeward, Angel* and *Of Time and the River* reappear, and, with one exception, every one of them is given the same name that he had

[4] Edward C. Aswell, "A Note on Thomas Wolfe," in *The Hills Beyond,* 377.

before. Aunt Louise, who taught Helen Gant music in the first novel, and who was actually Miss Grace Westall, is called Aunt Nell in "The Lost Boy." Here too she has taught Helen. There are a few characters who had not been used earlier. Old Crocker and his wife and their candy store figure in Wolfe's works for the first time. When he needed a new character, he could still reach far back into the past and select someone he had known and not described. Asheville still was an inexhaustible storehouse.

"The Lost Boy" is a story in four parts, the first of which is a description of Grover on the square and of Crocker's attempt to swindle him out of three one-cent stamps. Wolfe's technique mingles all the simplicity of his account of the murder in "The Return of the Prodigal" with some of the lyricism used to describe the youth of Eugene in *Look Homeward, Angel.* There is a kind of subjectivity that Wolfe had not used before; the point of view is not himself, but his brother Grover Wolfe, who died when Tom was four years old. Probably the simple pathos that is so striking in the story was gained by Wolfe's use of his own childhood as well as the stories about Grover that he had heard his family tell.

The local Libya Hill newspaper in *You Can't Go Home Again* wrote that George Webber in his book *Home to Our Mountains* had "described the Square with a photographic eye," but Webber, and vicariously Wolfe, denied the charge. There were, he wrote, "a hundred items of variation." If Webber was right (and I do not believe he was), Wolfe is closer to fact in *The Hills Beyond* than in the *Angel.* The square as seen by Grover corresponds in every significant detail to the square as it was in the time of the story, 1903. The fire department, the streetcar, the cobblestone pavement, the courthouse bell, "the fountain pulsing with its plume," the Singer sewing machine place in the Legal Building, the music store, the candy shop, and the monument shop run by Mr. Wolfe—all these can be checked accurately in old photographs and the city directories. If "The Lost Boy" is a universal story of pathos and the "soul-sickening guilt that all the children, all the good men of the earth, have felt since Time began," it also represents a very particularized study of the details that Grover and Tom Wolfe knew as children.

The last three parts of "The Lost Boy" are stories of Grover narrated by the mother, Eliza Gant, the sister Helen, and the brother Eugene. Told in the same stream-of-conversation method that Wolfe used in "The Web of Earth," these sections describe not only Grover but also the person talking. Eliza tells how he was her most mature and intelligent child. Using the mother's rambling, disjointed manner of conversation, the sister describes an old family photograph and Grover's death. The date, the people in the picture, the house, and the clothes follow almost exactly a photograph of the Wolfe family. Yet this description is probably only a little more exact than the transcription of Mrs. Wheaton's talking and of her lyric memories and puzzlement about the past and its meaning.

The brother is Eugene, whose description of Grover is based on his memories of that long-ago trip to the St. Louis Fair in the summer of his fourth year. Remembering Grover's death of typhoid in St. Louis, Wolfe went back to that city in 1934 or 1935. He had to consult old maps in the fire department before he was able to find the house where Mrs. Wolfe had kept boarders and where Grover had died. The name of the street had been changed. Eugene finds the same house only after two pages of inquiry and searching. The theme of the story concerns the past of Grover and the hero. Grover cannot return to life, and Tom Wolfe or Eugene Gant cannot see "his own small face again, pooled in the dark mirror of the hall, and peer once more into the grave eyes of the child that he had been, and discover there in his quiet three-years' self the lone integrity of 'I'. . . ."

Gentlemen of the Press, probably written in 1930 or 1931,[5] is one of Wolfe's last attempts to use the form of the drama. As a scene in the city room of one of the Asheville newspapers in "a hot night in June, 1916," it expresses Wolfe's interest in Asheville, life at night, the goodness of men who seem to be roughnecks, the evil of so-called society people, and the horrors of war. The central motifs are a reporter's desire to write a great historical novel, satire on Asheville socialites, and the death of a lieutenant in the Lafayette Escadrille. The reporter's plot was to revolve around a legend that Abraham Lincoln was born in western North Carolina. John Preston Arthur in his history of that region, incidentally, gives nineteen long pages to speculation on this subject. Lieutenant Clifford McKinley Brownlow was a native of Altamont. The boys called him "Miss Susie," taunted him, and chased him home from school. "Is that," a reporter asks, "the way a hero's made?"

The strangest thing about this play is its anticipation of the material that went into *The Web and the Rock*. Aswell dated it in 1930 or 1931, and in manner it does seem to be of an early period. Yet the names of the characters are closely connected with those in the first novel of the Webber cycle. Pretty Polly, one of the vivid brief portraits in this novel, sings Bartlett's "A Dream" in a dreadful manner throughout the first part of the play: ". . . threels—mee-uh—and stuh-heels—mee-uh—and

5 *Ibid.*, 378.

luh-hulls—mee-uh—to r-r-r-rest. . . ." Policeman Matthews and Captain Crane, who first appeared in *The Web and the Rock,* are described at a fire in the Negro district. Did Wolfe have in mind Nebraska Crane and his father as early as 1931? There is, furthermore, a strange connection between some of the mountain grills of the novel and the socially elite in the play. The surnames of Sidney Purtle, Ira Dingley, Carl Hooton, and Reese McMurdie—the social and economic riffraff—appear again in the play. Mrs. S. Frederick Purtle, Leroy Dingley, Seth Hooton, and Nemo McMurdie are written about in the society columns of the newspaper. This seems to be something more than a strange coincidence of Wolfe's memory, yet surely he did not expect many readers to catch the satirical effect of this reversal of the social status of names in two little related works of art.

If *Gentlemen of the Press* has as its central characters the most urbane and cynical of Asheville's citizens, "Chickamauga" is a story about the most primitive and simple mountaineers of Buncombe County. Despite Great-uncle John's ninety-four years, there is an unfailing clearness and accuracy of memory in his description of Chickamauga that would have been creditable for any Gant, even Eliza herself. This is the story that Scott Fitzgerald had in mind when he advised Wolfe to write on more universal and cosmopolitan subjects. But Wolfe's derisive reply about the Lost Generation and his obvious admiration of the characters in "Chickamauga" indicate his deep appreciation for the mores, traditions, and history of his mother's mountain family. Perhaps this story is indicative of the forces that were causing Wolfe to turn to a novel covering the entire span of history in North Carolina. His uncle's memory enabled Wolfe to carry the story back to the Civil War and back still further to Uncle John's birth "at the Forks of the Toe River in 1842," and even to the birth of Webber's "grand-paw" in 1828.

The dominant themes of "Chickamauga" are the character of Uncle John and his kind, the love story of Jim Weaver, and the battle itself. The mountain idiom is a most excellent vehicle for all these. Through digressions on the fanatical Uncle Bacchus, on the mountaineer's attitude toward education, and on war's effect on a man, the love story moves simply yet relentlessly forward. The basic plot is the same situation as that developed much more sentimentally in Thomas Nelson Page's "Marse Chan," without all the tear-jerking of that work. Jim Weaver, a more realistic soldier than Page's Marse Chan, hates the war with a passion as strong as his love for Martha Patton. But he is killed in the charge at Chickamauga. John Pentland is as faithful to Jim and his memory as Marse Chan's old slave was to his master, even though the end of the modern story would have been unbearably unromantic for Page's nineteenth-century readers: "And I would go all through the war and go back home and marry Martha later on, and fellers like Poor Jim was layin' thar at Chickamauga Creek."

The account of the battle is presented as simply as the love story in the mountain language, which conveys throughout the rhythm of mountain speech without the fantastic dialect of such local colorists as Mary Noailles Murfree. Uncle John tells his story plainly and quietly, with emotion, certainly; but his feelings, unlike his memory, have been tempered by the passing of the years since the war. He uses the homely figures of speech that have been dominant in good Southern writing since the time of Gus Longstreet and Davy Crockett. The old Southern humorists' device of telling a tall tale quietly and with a straight face is used by Uncle John over and over: "And when I came back after the war was over I could a-stood by and seed a man murdered right before my eyes with no more feelin' than I'd have had fer a stuck hog. I had no more feelin' about human life than I had fer the life of a sparrer. I'd seed a ten-acre field so thick with dead men that you could have walked all over hit without steppin' on the ground a single time." The cedar thicket in which the battle of Chickamauga was fought "was so thick and dense you could a-took a butcher knife and drove in thar anywheres and hit would a-stuck." After the battle, "you could a-looked in thar anywheres with your naked eye and seed a black snake run a hundred yards away . . . you'd a-wondered how a hummin' bird the size of your thumbnail could a-flown through thar without bein' torn into pieces by the fire." When the commanding officer tried to check his Union forces, "hit was like tryin' to swim the Mississippi upstream on a bone-yard mule."

The possible sources of Wolfe's story of the terrible battle are, of course, the personal memories of Uncle John, Wolfe's own reading of history, and his imagination. To write a realistic narrative about an old man's recollections of his service as an enlisted man in the Civil War was Wolfe's purpose, and thus he had to give an extremely personal point of view and to avoid the usual accuracy and pedantry of the scholar-historian, as well as the glorification of self and cause that is to be found in the numerous memoirs that have been published about soldiers in the Civil War. Wolfe succeeded too well for the critic who is interested in comparing the use of fact in fiction. What his uncle actually saw in the battle and what he endured were perhaps quite different from what, more than seventy years later, he told Wolfe he had seen. Perhaps different battles became confused in his mind. Again and again, for example, he describes the cedar thicket in which Chickamauga was fought, but one historian's version of the war experiences of Uncle John's Twenty-ninth North Carolina Regiment refers to a cedar thicket near Murfreesboro without mentioning one at Chickamauga.

Usually a historian attempts to give an over-all view of a battle; Uncle John vividly tells about what he and Jim Weaver saw and some of the things they heard. Wolfe, then, does attain the proper perspective. His soldier is interested in the men and the terrain before him and in shooting the enemy and protecting his own skin, not in the over-all battle. Many details correspond to those given in such an account as Stanley F. Horn's in *The Army of Tennessee.* Robert Selph Henry in *The Story of the Confederacy* gives a brief historical description of the stretcher-bearers' picking up the wounded. Wolfe and his Uncle John must necessarily see different things in a different way. This single paragraph gives perhaps the best account of how history or an old man's memory becomes fiction: "You could see the nurses and the stretcher-bearers movin' through the woods, and each side huntin' fer hits dead. You could see them movin' in the smoke an' flames, an' you could see the dead men layin' there as thick as wheat, with their corpse-like faces an' black powder on their lips, an' a little bit of moonlight comin' through the trees, and all of hit more like a nightmare out of hell than anything I ever knowed before." Thus, "Chickamauga" is successful as much because it is a story about a mountaineer as because it is a story of a battle in the Civil War.

One of Wolfe's most drastic alterations of historical truth occurs in the account in "Chickamauga" of the battle of Stone

Mountain, "the queerest one of the whole war." Uncle John tells of the Yankee attack on the Confederates, who were on top of the mountain. The Southerners defended themselves by rolling stones and boulders down the steep sides: "We jest rolled those boulders down on 'em, and I tell you what, hit was an awful thing to watch. I never saw no worse destruction than *that* with guns and cannon during the whole war." Actually, there was fighting within a mile or so of the mountain, but none whatsoever on the mountain itself. Wolfe had visited it when he was in Atlanta a short time before he wrote the story,[6] and it made such an impression on him that either he imagined a battle took place upon this huge rock or he transferred some real battle to this setting.

Wolfe's preoccupation with the pioneer settlers of the mountains in western North Carolina was an early interest that became stronger with the passing years. "The Men of Old Catawba," in *From Death to Morning*, begins, in essay or short story form, a history of Wolfe's native state, but he must have been unsatisfied with its brevity. The same material is reworked in the fragment "The Hills Beyond," but developed much further. It begins with the settlement of Old Catawba by Hugh Fortescue, obviously one of Sir Walter Raleigh's explorers, and then describes the Lost Colony and Fortescue's futile search for these first settlers on his return. The remainder of the first chapter, "The Quick and the Dead," is an essay on the social and political conflict between the aristocratic East and the West, "this obscure country cousin, this uncouth hillbilly."

[6] From a conversation with Professor Glenn W. Rainey, of the Georgia Institute of Technology. When Wolfe heard that Gutzon Borglum was the sculptor of the Confederate memorial that was to be carved on the mountain, he was fascinated by the man's name. He kept repeating, "Borglum, borgle up a mountain."

Courtesy University of
North Carolina Photo Lab.

Thomas Wolfe as "Buck Gavin"
in his play
The Return of Buck Gavin.

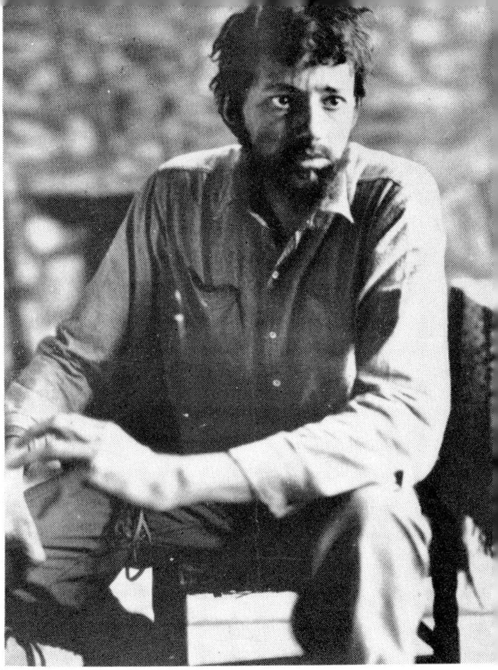

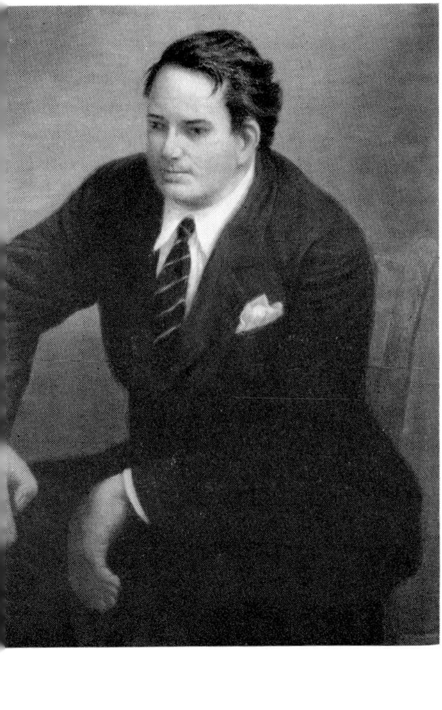

Reproduced by
permission of the artist

Portrait of Thomas Wolfe
by Douglas Gorsline.

The West wins under the leadership of Zachariah Joyner, genealogically in fiction one of the forebears of George Webber on his mother's side. This character is really based on the robust personality of the most flamboyant politician North Carolina ever produced, Civil War Governor Zebulon Baird Vance. Wolfe extended himself fictionally by breeding the Governor into the family line of his hero. Zachariah bursts on the scene with an obscene phrase about the lineage of his aristocratic opponent in the governor's race: "Good old yeoman stock, my ———!" From this point on Wolfe develops him as a man with the traits of a demagogue and the character of a statesman. He appeals to the red-necked, wool-hat voters by describing his own primitive background, indeed by exaggerating its primitivism, by using an illiterate dialect, the tall tale, the wisecrack told with a dead-pan face. That Wolfe's use of this common trait of the Southern politician was actually based on Vance's career is shown by Vance's writing in his old age about "the rough and unpolished ways which I so early affected as stepping stones to popularity among a rude mountain people."[7]

Wolfe had turned from the manner of the lyric writer of prose describing the artist as a young man in conflict with his environment to the manner of such early Southern writers as Longstreet, Johnson Jones Hooper, and George Washington Harris. He found the materials ready to hand. The great popularity that Governor Vance always enjoyed among North Carolinians was due as much to his readiness with a joke as it was to his integrity and continued respect for the "little fellow." Newspapers in the state still carry feature articles on Vance and the jokes that legends say he told. In his boyhood he wrote a

[7] Frontis W. Johnston, "Zebulon Baird Vance: A Personality Sketch," *North Carolina Historical Review*, Vol. XXX, No. 2 (April, 1953), 182.

parody of "The Old Oaken Bucket," beginning, "How dear to my heart are the pants of my childhood." In elementary school little Zeb once had to sit in a corner for swearing. Told to watch for a mouse that kept jumping out of a hole in the wall, Zeb caught it with a pair of tongs and yelled, "Damned if I didn't catch him!" He sold a jugful of pot liquor to two men who had asked him if he knew where they could buy some liquor. "Is that tobacco or what?" freshman Zeb was once asked by a senior who had just entered his room at the University of North Carolina. "It's what," he said, "help yourself." When Vance tried a case in court after he had become a lawyer, mobs of people flocked to hear his humorous performance. One deputy sheriff would turn his back to the judge who was anxious to keep silence. Near the end of one of Vance's jokes he would yell, "Silence in the courtroom," and then laugh first himself. The North Carolina Department of Archives and History still has an unpublished paper by Vance on "The Humorous Side of Politics."[8]

Wolfe created Zachariah Joyner and his father, William, as mythical frontier characters. William, who is nicknamed "Bear," with one blow broke a "blacksmith's ribs and caved in his side as one would crack a shell," had a fight with a bear, and "bit the nose off that big b'ar and chawed off both his years, and that b'ar was so tored up hit was a caution." He carried eight hundred pounds of leather on his back, refused to wear shoes even when company came, learned to read and write after forty years of illiteracy. Wolfe had collected, he said in *The Hills Beyond*, "more than eight hundred stories, anecdotes, and jokes" about Zack Joyner, "and of this number at least six hundred have the unmistakable ring—or *smack*—of

[8] *Ibid.*, 183.

truth"; and he claimed to have verified "three hundred as authentic beyond the shadow of a doubt." If a comparable collection of stories about Zeb Vance exists, however, it has not been described by any scholar. Wolfe's stories are more ribald than the feeble ones reprinted in the timid newspaper stories and the eulogistic speeches and biographies of the nineteenth century.

The speech Zack Joyner made in the Senate on building a bridge over Coon Creek in the Honorable Barnaby Bulwinkle's district is said by Wolfe to be certainly authentic, although it is not in the *Congressional Record.* When Zack assures the Senate that he "could ——— halfway across the stream," the vice president pounds his gavel and declares that "the Senator is out of order."

"Senator Joyner: Mr. President, sir, you are right. If I was *in* order, sir, I could ——— the whole way across it!"

True as this story is to the character of Governor Vance, he never made the speech, although he probably knew it and wished he had made it. Wolfe here used a very famous and obscene speech thought by most American historians who know it to have been made by State Senator Jefferson Davis (no relation to the president of the Confederacy), Senator Jones, or Representative Cassius M. Johnson in the Arkansas Legislature against the changing of the name of Arkansa*w* to Arkansas—in some versions, "Arkan's ass."[9] The portion Wolfe lifted is one of the most comic and decent sections of this florid and dramatic oration. Like many other college students in his time, Wolfe probably heard this speech and memorized it. It was so dramatically obscene, so the story goes, that all records of it

[9] Several versions of this speech are printed in James R. Masterson, *Tall Tales of Arkansaw* (Boston, Chapman and Grimes, 1943), 180–85, 352–58.

were expunged from the records of the Legislature. Although there are folklore versions remembered all over the country and circulating on smuggled, obscene records, no folklore quarterly has ever dared reprint it. Zachariah Joyner is a more magnificent governor than Zeb Vance simply because Wolfe used every tall tale he could remember in adding to the legend. Zack's brother Rufus, he says, is so mean that "he wouldn't ——— down a preacher's throat if his guts were on fire." Every child who ever heard a joke in the mountains thirty years ago knew this hyperbole.

Together, Bear and Zack Joyner are the central figures of the first five chapters of *The Hills Beyond* and Wolfe's account of the early history of North Carolina. They are embodiments of the frontier and mountain legends of America, and to create them Wolfe drew from his mother's family as well as from the family of Governor Vance. The parallels to both are somewhat vague, much more than in Wolfe's early books, but they are still recognizable. Mrs. Julia Wolfe told Edward Aswell that of all the Joyners described in *The Hills Beyond* she could place only old Bill Joyner and Miss Hattie in her family tree.[10] Yet both these characters are likenesses of persons in the Vance line also, besides being drawn from Wolfe's general knowledge of frontier and mountain lore. Miss Hattie, who is the "love child" of Bear Joyner, and whose obscure birth is never mentioned in her own family, is quite as lusty a character as her father and brother. She is, Wolfe writes, "more like Zachariah in her ribald humor than any of the others." Although Mrs. Wolfe could recognize her, she was also closely modeled on Celia Vance, who once shot a hole in the corner of the Vance home while she was trying to do the manual of arms

[10] Aswell, "A Note on Thomas Wolfe," in *The Hills Beyond*, 385.

with a six-foot-long shotgun.[11] She also resembles Hannah Vance, another of Zack's sisters. Once, when a snobbish lady at a fashionable party sneered and purred that "no perfect lady wears a shoe larger than a number three," Zack asked Hannah what size she wore. "Number seven, brother," came in a loud answer.[12]

The Joyner home is an exact description of the still-standing home built by Zeb Vance's father, although the house is now almost a ruin, not "kept piously by the State Historical Commission," as Wolfe asserts. Judge Robert Joyner, Zack's brother, is lame like Robert Vance, the third son of the family. The Vances grew up on a farm near Asheville, and they had relatives in Burnsville, also the home of many of Mrs. Wolfe's kinsmen. Wolfe's fusion of the two family trees was, therefore, an easy as well as a rewarding task. One might draw numerous other minor parallels between Wolfe's Joyners and the Vances.

Theodore Joyner dominates the fifth and sixth chapters of *The Hills Beyond*, and for him Wolfe has little admiration and much contempt. His social, educational, and militaristic pretenses are shown when he builds his school on Hogwart Heights, rechristens the hill Joyner Heights, names his school the Joyner Heights Academy, and renames it the Joyner Heights Military Academy. Theodore, his brother Zack says, "*leaps* in where God Almighty crawls." He trains some cadets for the Civil War, and "in April 1861, the entire enrollment of the academy marched away to battle with Theodore at their head."

After the war, Theodore becomes the " 'Southern Colonel-plumed knight' kind of man" and makes a "folk-religion" of the cause of the South. He builds up his social and military

11 *Asheville Citizen*, September 4, 1927.
12 *Asheville Citizen-Times*, October 15, 1933.

myth, while Zack tears it down with jokes. Theodore's wife refuses for a long time to accept the society of the Willets (really the Vanderbilts), because they were not born in the Virginia aristocracy. (The prototype of this haughty character was really a descendant of the Worths, a family prominent in North Carolina.)

Of Theodore's military prowess his brother Zack is derisive: "So far as I know, he is the only officer in the history of the Confederacy who possesses the distinction of having been shot in the seat of the pants by one of his own sharpshooters, while stealthily and craftily reconnoitering his own breastworks in search of any enemy who was at that time nine miles away and marching in the opposite direction!"

For this Joyner, Wolfe used as a prototype Colonel Robert Bingham, head of the once glorious but now defunct Bingham Military Academy. When Wolfe finished college at the University of North Carolina, he turned down a job as teacher at the Bingham school, but there was no closer relationship between the author and the headmaster. Wolfe did not even attend the school as a child. Yet the Colonel was the embodiment of the false romantic legend about the Civil War and Southern chivalry. Like Theodore Joyner, he loved to deliver florid pronouncements and orations on the greatness of the cause. He wrote that as a war prisoner of the Northern troops he had endured a high temperature of 140 degrees, and in the winter he had shivered, man though he was, at 30 below. The written reminiscences of the Colonel were the subjects of Wolfe's satire.

In this history Wolfe was using all the native lore that he knew and writing a conglomeration that is much harder to trace to its sources than any other of his writings about Asheville. When he created Gustavus Adolphus Joyner, the son of Theodore, he returned to the lyric style of *Look Homeward, Angel* and probably again to memories of his own childhood. Even Wolfe's ideas about the mountains grow out of the concrete and spring from his feelings when he was a child. After giving his theory of the effect of the mountains on men, he exemplified his beliefs by describing the magnificent view from Hogwart (really Bingham) Heights, where Wolfe as a child must have enjoyed the same view as that seen by Gustavus Adolphus in *The Hills Beyond*. One who reads the book while standing on the Heights can see the detailed accuracy of Wolfe's geographical descriptions.

This accuracy is a good cause for speculation on the difference between the real and the artistic as Wolfe created it even in the last book about his home town. On pages 282–84 of *The Hills Beyond* there is not an item that is not factual description. The difference is that Wolfe has added emotional and lyrical content to character and scene, and Gustavus Adolphus is a combination of Eugene, George, and Tom. The process is essentially the same as it was in the first novel.

The new objectivity is not less dependent on fact, is not less subjective; it is just as dependent on autobiography. What then causes the big difference about which Edward Aswell has written so much? There is in the last book more historical and more artistic association of more sources, and that is all. Wolfe did not create himself in this work, but he created characters a little more unlike himself than his early heroes had been and then put himself in them. Here is a kind of development and trend that would have determined Wolfe's artistic future. He would have succeeded, perhaps, in removing his characters farther and farther from himself. Possibly, however, he would have lost more than he would have gained.

When Wolfe used himself and Eugene and George to create the new character of "Silk" Joyner, as Gustavus Adolphus was called, he retained some of the lyricism and imagination of those characters, but his objectivity and creativeness show in a new element. Silk Joyner is a dreamer, but unlike Tom Wolfe in fact and fiction, he is a man who is looking for advantages. "His vision of life was utterly utilitarian, and the only utility he recognized was that which applied to himself." Wolfe's growing practice of combining divergent things when he wrote was enabling him to create a greater variety of fictional characters. There is, however, a loss also: Silk Joyner is inferior in conception to Eugene and George.

In chapter VII the "stranger whose sermon was brick" comes to Libya Hill, and thus Wolfe used for the third time Mr. W. O. Wolfe's settling in the mountain town. When John Webber appears on the scene, Wolfe approached in his history the era that he had already written about twice in *Look Homeward, Angel* and *The Web and the Rock*. If he was to follow again the theme of a boy's love and admiration of his father, he again needed a youth to idolize John Webber. The world of Silk Joyner prevented the development of the kind of character that George and Eugene had been. Wolfe therefore created still another child to play the autobiographical role. Edward, the son of Judge Robert Joyner, makes his appearance in the very chapter that describes John Webber's arrival.

The last part of *The Hills Beyond* becomes in the character of Edward another lyrical account of childhood in a small town. As a fragment on an old subject, it is not so fresh and artistic a work as Wolfe's earlier stories of his life in Asheville, but it might have approached the others if Wolfe had been able to complete and revise it. Living in the South some years earlier than Eugene and George, Edward has different experiences. With his ideas about brick and the permanence a building should have, John Webber rebuilds Libya Hill, and Edward thinks of time in terms of "Before Webber and After Webber." "And because that earlier time—B. W.—" Wolfe writes, "is the harder to recapture [Wolfe could not use his own memory], we shall begin by trying to describe it."

Thus, he launches into a summary of the history of Asheville and its "old settlers" from the time when it was "little more than a crossroads country village." The courthouse bell that haunts Edward Joyner, the courthouse itself as the center of the community life, its architecture and its smell of sweat, urine, and tobacco juice, the coming of the first train to Libya Hill in 1884—these and the other details that Wolfe uses in his history are directly and accurately based on some of the most interesting aspects of the historical development of Asheville as a mountain resort town.

The central fact of the town's existence in *The Hills Beyond* has been the Civil War. Judge Joyner has an "instinctive and deep-rooted feeling against the War" and a great reticence in conversations about it, but Edward is so much intrigued by it that he spends his time on accounts of the war but flunks history. Old Looky Thar, a professional veteran and one of the chief protagonists of the glories of the war, becomes one of Wolfe's most comic characters. He uses the hole in the roof of his mouth that was his injury in the war to win respect, charity, and any argument in which he engages. Judge Joyner, on the other hand, succeeds for years in keeping Edward, his own son, from knowing that he is a cripple. Indeed, the boy learns of his father's losing a leg in the war only when he reads about it in "an account of the Battle of Spottsylvania by one of the Generals in Hancock's command who had been present at the fight." Apparently the most plausible source of the long quotation that Wolfe uses is General Nelson A. Miles's *Serving the Republic*, but the small number of similar statements in fiction and in the General's memoirs probably indicates that Wolfe himself wrote the passage describing the heroism of Robert Joyner.

The fragment "The Hills Beyond" ends half a century after Edward read the story of his father in battle. It ends with the son's memory of that lost day, "of each blade, each leaf, each flower," of the courthouse, the loafers, the wagons, the brothels, and the whores. The last paragraph is as lyrical as the opening page of *Look Homeward, Angel*: "Time passing as men pass who never will come back again . . . and leaving us, Great God, with only this . . . knowing that this earth, this time, this life, are stranger than a dream."

Thus, Wolfe had come full circle. He began and ended with a lyric description of his own life and his memories, and seldom, indeed, had he ever written of things conjured wholly from the visions of his mind. Altamont, Libya Hill, and every book that he wrote are autobiographical accounts of Tom Wolfe and Asheville. Surely no self-exiled author has ever dwelt mentally so much in the land of his origins. Even in the last phases of his career as an author, even when he had quit recording the town, his family, and himself with photostatic accuracy and poetic frenzy, he still created no new towns, people, and states. If there are composite characters and Joyners and Pentlands who are alien to his mother's family, these fictional figures are still based on reality. The statistical facts given in round numbers are true in spirit. No historian with all the pedantry he could marshal has ever pictured the subject matter with greater spiritual truth. Yet Wolfe was right when he implied that one cannot create fiction merely by telling the facts about his town and the people. One sort of history is that seen with a point of view, with a bias, with subjectivity. History is as much connotation as denotation and fact. A number is an abstraction, but its literal meaning to each reader is concretely personal.

8. Prodigal Home Again

With a strange and compelling attraction, North Carolina and the South remained throughout the years the milieu and the conditioning element in the works of Thomas Wolfe. *Look Homeward, Angel* had been written in London and the North, but it had recorded Asheville with a keenness of vision, perception, and memory denied to lifelong residents. After its violent reception, Wolfe became for seven years an expatriate, like his friends Fitzgerald and Lewis, those escapees from the devastating barrenness they found in Midwestern life. Whereas members of the Lost Generation had discovered in Paris merely a more sensational and lurid way of being lost, Wolfe discovered the necessity of belief. Following the great chagrin and crushing disappointment caused by his townsmen's attitude toward his first book, he felt more than ever when he was in Paris "the bitter ache of homelessness, a desperate longing for America, an overwhelming desire to return."[1]

His homesickness for Asheville and the South seem to have been a controlling emotion during his years away. There was tragedy in his discovery that he could not return home again, and all his works in one way and another looked back to that

[1] *The Story of a Novel,* 31.

Asheville which at times, perhaps, he had wished to reject. George Webber's book had looked *Home to Our Mountains*, and the last work Wolfe wrote was about *The Hills Beyond*, which includes a story on "The Return of the Prodigal." When Wolfe visited his sister, Mrs. Ralph Wheaton, in Washington, they would cross the Potomac and go a short distance south of Mason's mythical line, and Wolfe would exclaim again and again to his sister, "Great God, Mabel, to think I'm on Southern soil." His decision that spiritually he could not go home to western North Carolina was made after years of effort and trial, not with the publication of *Look Homeward, Angel*.

The changes in Wolfe's traditional, cultural, and regional loyalty were occurring over the years when Asheville also was changing its attitude toward this famous son who had seemed a great disaster at first. After the first white heat of anger, there began a steady progression from rejection to forgetting and finally to adulation. The change from scandal to glory and fame is not yet entirely accomplished, perhaps, but Asheville now should blush as much for excessive praise as for the original condemnation.

That the bitterness was not extremely short-lived is shown by the variety of articles appearing in North Carolina newspapers the next spring after *Look Homeward, Angel* came out in the fall. Writing in the *Charlotte Observer*, May Johnston Avery in March was still digging up startling facts about the first impetuous reactions, but she also recorded the trend toward forgiveness and acceptance. Except for details, Asheville's position is virtually summarized in her lengthy subhead: "Some Think He Ought to Be Spanked for His Impertinence in So Vividly Portraying Them, At Times With an Uncomplimentary Brush—Others Willing to Forgive the Sting of Ridicule

Because of the Greatness of the Book He Has Written."[2]

Wolfe's expectation that he would receive from the local paper an invitation to defend his novel was fulfilled in May of 1930, when the *Asheville Times*, one of his severest critics, asked him about his attitude toward his home town. Even the invitation itself was perhaps an indication of a mounting wave of public opinion in his favor. Unlike George Webber, who fictionally wrote and tore up his answer, Wolfe wrote and mailed a reply. Intended to allay the criticism and to soothe ruffled tempers, the letter is a declaration of faith in his native environs: "I am proud of my family, and I still consider Asheville my home. New York certainly is not. I like it, but it is a giant of steel and stone far different from the open spaces where a man can plant his feet on caressing earth and breathe." Declaring that he was writing with all his heart, Wolfe said that he did not want his friends to think of him as an exile. He considered Ashevillians "the heart of America." He disagreed with Sinclair Lewis: "Some writers like Sinclair Lewis have missed the meat of the small town, anyway. Although people recognize his characters, his towns were painted as drab and dull. I do not consider them so, I mean typically American towns. Life is there in all its fullness."[3] That he was willing to extend himself and his feelings in this letter is shown by his wavering and by his private letters. On June 2, in a letter to his brother Fred, Wolfe indicated his variable attitude by writing that any homesickness he ever had was not for the town, "but for the great and marvelous hills of North Carolina in which I was fortunate enough to be born, and in which Asheville had the good sense to get built. My feeling is for the

[2] *Charlotte Observer*, March 30, 1930.

[3] *Asheville Times*, May 4, 1930.

land, my blood kin, and a few people—beyond that I care very little."[4]

Several days after the paper published this letter from Wolfe, it carried an impartial editorial about how *Look Homeward, Angel* was second only to La Farge's *Laughing Boy* in the competition for the Pulitzer prize. It was not soon enough, however, for all the bitterness to be gone, and the news was accompanied by an unnecessary confession that the *Times* itself "has no admiration for the class of fiction to which the book belongs."[5] There is notably the absence of the charge of autobiography and scandal.

That long period of waiting between the appearance of a successful first novel and its successor and all the charges that a novelist has "written himself out" in his first book were worse for Wolfe than for most authors. If there was in the outside world doubt and lack of finality of judgment about *Look Homeward, Angel,* Asheville was beset by intensified doubt and speculation. Sometimes the papers and the people treated Wolfe as the celebrity he had become in the outside world; sometimes they wrote of him as one who had gained notoriety by an infamous deed. All during this period, *Of Time and the River* was in preparation, although he worked on it under a number of titles before he made the final choice. In August of 1931, the *Citizen* announced *October Fair* and in the first paragraph gave assurance to local citizens that "they will not appear as characters." (They did.) Mrs. Wolfe was quoted as promising that the book would "show a softening of the cynicism revealed in the first book."[6]

[4] *Letters,* 230.

[5] *Asheville Times,* May 15, 1930.

[6] *Asheville Citizen,* August 9, 1931.

That strange fate that followed Wolfe and caused utterly sensational things to happen to him and his fame began to account for a number of local stories about him. In Germany in 1931, he was involved in a beer hall brawl in which he received a dangerous cut on the head when he was hit by a thrown beer bottle. The incident is rather accurately described as happening to Eugene Gant in *Of Time and the River.* In its announcement of *October Fair,* the *Citizen* printed a fairly long feature story of the brawl as it had been told to his mother, and its tone is like that of most sentimental journalistic articles that attempt to make the local boy look good. Also there was a description of the "generous reception [of *Look Homeward, Angel*] from critics in this country and abroad" and of its being barred in the Irish Free State.[7] Although the writer calls attention to the presence in the public library of *The Return of Buck Gavin,* discreetly he fails to mention the absence of the *Angel* from the same shelves.

Stories of Wolfe's activities began to appear with some regularity at this time. If his local public were not admirers, the *Citizen* was at least trying to mold a feeling of tolerance. In October it published a story about Wolfe's attending a meeting at the University of Virginia, an informal forum on "The Southern Author in Relation to His Public." Wolfe, unfortunately, did not join such writers as Ellen Glasgow, Stark Young, Donald Davidson, Paul Green, and Willa Cather. Had he gone, certainly he would have been a focal point; no one had a relationship with his public more sensational and promiscuous. The same article in the *Citizen* which announced that he was to attend the meeting also discussed his possible new *October Fair.* The paper was interested in the topic of

[7] *Ibid.*

the meeting as it applied to the local author. The projected new novel was still not a palliative for the sickened minds of Asheville: "Whether he will again enter the intimate recesses of local character sketching is not known," the *Citizen* expressed its fears. "That, also, has been rumored."[8]

On March 15, 1932, *October Fair* was again announced as being almost ready for publication, and this time there was the added news, and to Asheville the dreaded omen, that there was a source for the new character, Bascom Hawke. According to Wolfe's mother, the story "A Portrait of Bascom Hawke" would "feature Mr. Wolfe's impressions of the peculiarities and habits of a friend a man [*sic*] who once lived in Asheville." The papers, seldom silent on any issue in connection with Wolfe, were carrying numerous and rather long articles about his short stories. Eight days later came the news that Scribner's had selected "The Portrait of Bascom Hawke" in the five-thousand-dollar prize contest.[9] This time the reporter had read the story and found that "Wolfe's subject is thought to be a man born in Western North Carolina [his uncle H. A. Westall, of Boston]. The story is based on many true facts concerning the man who is still practicing [law] at more than 70 years of age." Perhaps fearing returning winds after the eye of the hurricane had passed, the paper remained noncommittal. There is not even a condemnation of the autobiography or of Wolfe's description of his Uncle Bascom's parsimony.

People in Asheville continued to watch the appearance of Wolfe's short stories with a skeptical and fearful eye. After a short and factual account of the publication of the novelette "The Web of Earth" in the middle of June, 1932,[10] a week later

8 *Ibid.*, October 25, 1931.
9 *Ibid.*, March 23, 1932.
10 *Ibid.*, June 18, 1932.

the *Citizen* ran a feature story that expressed for the first time public condemnation of Wolfe by a member of his family. "Mother of Tom Wolfe is Not Pleased with Her Son's Last Story," the headline read, and the article quoted Mrs. Wolfe as saying that her son should never have written the story because of the possibility that it might hurt the feelings of the relatives of the deceased people whom Wolfe had used as characters. Even Mrs. Wolfe disliked the story because it brought back "unpleasant memories."[11] This reaction caused the paper itself to have its unpleasant memories of the local sensation caused by *Look Homeward, Angel* and of how "the weaknesses of the various characters in the work were especially stressed." Was "The Web of Earth" a prediction of new terrors in the novel to come? "Local persons wonder," the *Citizen* said, "will Asheville again be on parade?"

If "The Web of Earth" dealt with individual local scandals and crimes, "Boom Town," which appeared first in 1934 as a short story and later in *You Can't Go Home Again*, was a description of the great communal sin of the community. The evil of speculation and materialism is hard to see in oneself, until the dire consequences have occurred. Then the guilty individual or community is more regretful than repentant, and the guilty one believes that he is a tragic victim of unfortunate circumstances rather than a sinner paying for his ways of evil. Such was the attitude of the *Citizen* toward "Boom Town." Failing to see Wolfe's description of Asheville as typical of booming America, the writer for the *Citizen* dwelt on the local angle exclusively. In this account there seems to be a sneer even in factual statements. "Boom Town," the paper said, "is printed in the May American Mercury as a piece of fiction,"

[11] *Ibid.*, June 26, 1932.

but "older residents here may be able to recognize a few, if not all, the characters in this story. . . ."[12] Besides autobiography, there was also "the same naked, biting style that was evident in his former work." This time the present reality was so bitter that the reporter did not speculate on *October Fair* and the evil things to come.

The hopes and fears that Thomas Wolfe had said all he had to say in *Look Homeward, Angel* were forgotten in 1935, when *Of Time and the River* was published in March and *From Death to Morning* in November. These two volumes proved that he had to be reckoned with in the years to come, and during attempts to adjust themselves to the situation, the papers published views that ranged from a violent bitterness to glowing appreciation of native talent. Some of the adverse reviews in this year are almost comical because of their hysterical determination to be as vicious as possible, and at the same time feature stories marked by an almost foolish adulation began to appear. These opposing attitudes mark a significant turning point, and it was only two more years until Wolfe, because of the changes in his own attitude and the town's, was able to make the long-delayed trip home. The first significant article of the year was an editorial that quoted Peter Monro Jack's review of *Of Time and the River* in the *New York Times Book Review*. Of particular interest in Asheville was Jack's wondering "if some of this autobiographical fiction material has its proper place in even such a series as Mr. Wolfe is writing so powerfully at white heat."[13] But the conclusion disregarded the local and, in a nonplused and puzzled way, attempted to arrive at objectivity: "Some of the things that he writes may

12 *Ibid.*, April 26, 1934.
13 *Ibid.*, March 12, 1935.

fill many with disgust," the writer said, "but how else shall we take a clearly great writer except for what he is?"

In April the *Citizen* published an article about Wolfe's popularity at Western Carolina Teachers College. Praise of his writings by the members of the English department was quoted, yet one note of dissent was found even in this glowing collection of tributes. One member of the faculty library board at the institution had objected to the mere presence of *Look Homeward, Angel* in the library.[14] In June the *Citizen-Times* even welcomed a student's youthful critical effusions on *Of Time and the River*,[15] and "Asheville's cosmic novelist" was the magnificent title given Wolfe by the *Citizen* in August. Professor Phillips Russell, then associate professor of English at the University of North Carolina, made a speech in Asheville and lashed out at those who termed Wolfe "not quite a gentleman." The outraged Professor Russell said that such opposition as Wolfe had encountered always accompanied a move from aristocracy to democracy, from romance to realism.[16]

The other attitude of that year is best typified by Weimar Jones's most vicious review of *Of Time and the River*. Deficient in plot, action, continuity, humor, and characterization, that book, in Jones's opinion, "has almost none of the things that ordinarily go into the making of a successful novel. . . . It moves at a snail's pace." Although he found one comic incident, "after he had laughed, he had the guilty feeling one has who applauds at the wong time."[17] The characterizations were marked by distorted and repetitious caricature, and the reviewer thought *Of Time and the River* "the work of a man who is warped."

[14] *Ibid.*, April 7, 1935.
[15] *Asheville Citizen-Times*, June 2, 1935.
[16] *Asheville Citizen*, October 12, 1935.
[17] *Ibid.*, April 21, 1935.

Even the superb style when read aloud revealed "its verboseness, its attempts at rhetorical emphasis, and its repetition."

In 1937, Wolfe came home again. He had, however, spent a number of years in going home on imaginative journeys to gather material for his books as well as to face the problems that awaited him in the community. The very perils of the imagination, indeed, were a major reason for his staying away. He had "forgotten time" (and thereby responsibility to the place of his origin), he says in *The Story of a Novel,*[18] and he had been "drugged there in the drowsy fumes of some green country of the witches' magic [in the world away from Asheville], with something in me dark and full of grief I could not quite remember." When Wolfe examined himself completely out of fiction in the summer of 1935, when he gave at the University of Colorado the speech that became *The Story of a Novel,* he reached some startling conclusions, and perhaps these thoughts were what led him home two years later. He decided that he had "grown old in some evil and enchanted place." "I had," he admitted, "betrayed my home, my friends, my people in the duties of some solemn and inviolable trust—and suddenly [in imagination] I was home again, and *silence* was my answer!"[19]

Again what had appeared as fact was recounted in his writing as fiction. Written in the last year of his life after he had been home, and published in the posthumous *The Hills Beyond,* "The Return of the Prodigal" has two parts: "The Thing Imagined," and "The Real Thing." In the first, Eugene Gant shows Thomas Wolfe's obsession with return: "And through all these seven years when he did not go back, his thoughts went back forever."[20] In the story of the imaginary return,

18 *The Story of a Novel,* 64.
19 *Ibid.,* 66.
20 *The Hills Beyond,* 108.

however, he does not mention his reception by the town. In "The Real Thing," Eugene recalls that "time passes, and puts halters to debate. And one day, when his seven years were up, he packed his bag and started out for home."[21] This supposedly fictitious presentation of the facts of Wolfe's coming home shows him smothered by the attentions of Rotarians, sincere friends, people seeking his artistic advice, girls wanting to type for him, and all sorts of people. One of his friends tells him that the only angry Ashevillians are those not described in *Look Homeward, Angel.*

The way to Asheville began with a trip to the South, but not home. First he went to New Orleans in January of 1937, then to the University of North Carolina and Raleigh. Here he made a speech to Professor Russell's creative writing class, and a student duly sent an account to the *Asheville Citizen.* The old subject was on his mind, and he tried to distinguish for the class the difference between Altamont and Asheville: "If you are from North Carolina," he said, "you have to use North Carolina clay to model a figure. Then the people of North Carolina recognize the clay and think that they recognize the figure. . . . The people thought a writer was a person who came from way over there and who said 'hocus pocus' and pulled a book out of the air."[22]

There is no license in "The Return of the Prodigal." For Tom Wolfe it was almost as simple, once the time came, as Eugene Gant's packing his bag and starting out for home. From Roanoke, Virginia, on April 28, 1937, he wrote his mother that he was on his way to Asheville and that he expected to arrive there after a few days with relatives in Burnsville. "It will be

21 *Ibid.*, 120.
22 *Asheville Citizen,* January 31, 1937.

a very strange experience, I think, coming back to Asheville after all this time." A week later he was back in New York, but planning to make another trip and hoping that he could get "peace and seclusion" at a cabin in the mountains. A month later he was again planning to leave "some time next week for Asheville." Altogether that summer he spent about ten weeks in his home town.

The two returns of the prodigal Wolfe were like "The Real Thing" of the prodigal Gant. There were reconciliations, and the lion hunters of Asheville proved themselves little different from those who had mobbed him in the North. He was photographed and interviewed, and, like a good Rotarian, he spoke to the civic clubs.[23] He told a reporter from the *Citizen* that he had been homesick in New York and Europe, "that he was sorry if he had displeased anyone," and that "a man is strongly attracted to the earth he comes from."[24] In a talk to the American Business Club, which would have been a proper subject for his satire, he described his happiness "to again breath [*sic*] the mountain air and see the mountainous skyline," and he expressed his desire to settle in Asheville.[25] Dutifully he told a banquet gathered to launch a drive for funds to build an auditorium that there was a "cultural and spiritual need" for the project.[26]

If the *Citizen's* reporters are to be believed, Wolfe was happy at home even though the hullabaloo around him kept him from writing anything except "The Party at Jack's," now part of *You Can't Go Home Again.* Just after Wolfe left in Septem-

23 George W. McCoy, "Asheville and Thomas Wolfe," *North Carolina Historical Review,* Vol. XXX, No. 2 (April, 1953), 212.

24 *Asheville Citizen,* May 4, 1937.

25 *Ibid.*

26 *Asheville Citizen,* August 31, 1937.

ber, the *Citizen* announced that he had " 'loved it all.' " " 'To be back among my own people has been one of the most thrilling and most memorable experiences I have ever known,' he stated. 'I wouldn't have missed it for anything. I have wanted for a long time to get back home. I had been away so long that it was beginning to haunt me. This summer has satisfied something in me that has wanted fulfillment for years.

'I am realy [*sic*] grateful from the bottom of my heart for the kind reception of this summer.' "[27]

His stay in Asheville was a round of backslapping and civic meetings, and everyone seemed pleased. For the city and for Wolfe it had been a strange time. Although there had been threats and dread forebodings, and although Wolfe himself had been hurt and angry in the years before he came, no evil note was sounded. People who met him on the street told him and wished to tell him that he could come home. Some middle-aged ladies still brag of having had a date with him, although they sometimes admit that he was so drunk that he could not have remembered them. Tact was a good oil slick on the surface, and if ill wishes lurked in the depths of the jovial city, they have not yet been described.

Wolfe, however, had not been altogether pleased. He wrote his friend and teacher Mrs. Roberts that he was disturbed; that the people had gone to the dogs; that although he was moved, he had discovered the impossibility of going home; that the civic clubs he had addressed were "howlingly funny," yet tragic and pathetic; and that he had developed more compassion and understanding.[28]

27 *Ibid.*, September 3, 1937.
28 Wolfe, "Writing Is My Life," *Atlantic Monthly*, Vol. CLXXIX, No. 2 (February, 1947), 57.

These were his views until his death. His last letter to his sister Mrs. Wheaton, May 10, 1938, described Asheville as a "ruined and defeated town . . . full of ruined and defeated people." But ruin and defeat had not destroyed his sympathy: "If you think I am happy about this," he wrote his sister, "you do me an injustice. After all, it was my town, I was born there, and some of the people I care for most on earth still live there. But I found out last summer that you can't go home again, and now I know why."[29] He told his friend R. P. Harris that on his trip to Asheville he learned "that being forgiven was almost worse than being damned. Did you ever have just too much hospitality."[30]

In February of 1938, he was interested in getting information to help him complete a portrait of the city, and he asked Mrs. Roberts to send him materials. The last months of his life, after the trip to Asheville, were spent in writing a book on how the prodigal could not return. In July of 1938, while making a note-taking tour of the Northwest, Thomas Wolfe took pneumonia. After a desperate sickness, a nightmarish trip across the continent, and a brain operation in Johns Hopkins Hospital, he died there on September 15, 1938. The threat of Tom Wolfe had vanished, and now he could go home only for the funeral. Sincerely stricken, Asheville sorrowfully prepared its memories for the occasion, and virtually all controversy was buried with his body.

On the day of his death the *Times* that had once been so vitriolic was warm in praise and elegiac in tone. Wolfe, the paper sadly declared, was not "personally as cynical" as he seemed in his writings; he was, indeed, "warm-hearted, often

[29] *Letters*, 761.
[30] *Asheville Citizen*, September 21, 1938.

friendly to a fault."[31] Inspired by memories and attempting to imitate his genius, several Ashevillians, one of them a minister, published poems in the papers on his death; and editorials in imitative Wolfean rhetoric appeared. On the day after his death, the *Citizen* wrote a detailed and laudatory and somewhat sentimental story about his childhood. "He was a real boy," the writer said. Seen in the new light, the old charges seemed ridiculous: "A writer is thinking about the story that is within him," the journalist quoted Wolfe, "and not about any particular town or any particular person." And he had been a true Southerner. His spitting upon the South and fowling his own nest—these had been misinterpretations, now not to be mentioned at all. Why, had he not been, on his last trip home, "a firm believer in the South"?[32] And hadn't he been delighted at coming home and at the warmness of his reception? In an editorial the city mourned "the passing of genius" and grieved "much more deeply the death of a son."[33] The community had come to view with "glowing satisfaction," the editorialist continued, "the sensitive, high-spirited, great-hearted, home-loving, home-town boy."

The greatest dignity and constancy in all the tumultuous relationship between Wolfe and Asheville have been exhibited by George W. McCoy, who, as a newspaper reporter and a close friend of Wolfe, tried always to mediate between the city and the writer. That first favorable review of *Look Homeward, Angel* in Asheville had been written by the lady who was to marry McCoy, and after Wolfe's death, McCoy himself wrote "A Giant Has Fallen," a famous obituary of praise with-

[31] *Asheville Times*, September 15, 1938.
[32] *Asheville Citizen*, September 16, 1938.
[33] *Ibid.*

out sentimentality. "Large of body, robust of mind, he was a man who matched our mountains."[34]

The most complete change of attitude is evident in the obituary that Jonathan Daniels wrote for the Raleigh *News and Observer* and reprinted in *The Saturday Review of Literature.* Daniels had forgotten that Wolfe had "gone the way of rebels"; that there had been a "reign of terror in his talent"; that he had turned in fury upon the South and his native state; that the life in *Look Homeward, Angel* was "stirred only by the raw lusts for food and drink and sex and property"; that the characters in the work were "prostitutes . . . and dope-fiends, drunken doctors, tuberculars, newsboys and teachers"; and that there was too much "blood and sex and cruelty." But in 1938, Daniels believed that "Wolfe drew his land as it was and wise men in it rejoiced for the drawing." Wolfe had set down Asheville as he had known it, Daniels now believed, "in love, in contempt, in beauty and in ugliness." The portrayal was passionate, sensitive, and sharp, and it was a "portrayal full of love." Daniels was chagrined that the world saw Wolfe's novels as "undisciplined and formless." "In his lifetime," the editor lamented, "his books were banned from the library of his native town of Asheville which in time's own irony came proudly to claim him after he was dead. That is an old custom."[35]

They buried the hatchet when they buried Wolfe, and now that he was gone—to change the figure—the sheep could appear in the clothing of Wolfe's followers. Those who had attacked him most also mourned him most.[36] Thirty-nine Ashevillians and twelve persons from foreign places served as hon-

[34] *Ibid.*, September 18, 1938.
[35] Raleigh *News and Observer*, September, 1938.
[36] *Asheville Citizen*, September 19, 1938.

orary pallbearers. People who could find no room in the church stood outside during the funeral, and hundreds more attended the interment.

After death, a prophet in his own country is respected, sometimes because there is no longer the threat of exposure and prophecy. Asheville had many motives in improving its attitudes toward Wolfe. There was, first of all, the tourist trade, and having a great writer as a native son never hurt any town that yearned for the foreign dollar. In that respect even the scandal had helped. Another significant cause of change was the activity of Wolfe's sincere friends and of those who developed an honest liking for his works. These people earnestly tried to stop further bitterness and misunderstanding. "We can take our Wolfe or leave it alone," the *Citizen* once insisted, "according to individual tastes in reading."[37] Perhaps most important of all was the opiate of forgetfulness. Transient emotions may be considered long in dying even if they linger just ten years. Citizens had moved away from the town, they had died, new people had come in, and others had merely aged ten years and forgotten in the process.

In February of 1939, the manuscript of *Look Homeward, Angel* was sold for seventeen hundred dollars, which was given to help the Spanish loyalists. An effusive editorial writer in the *Citizen* declared emotionally that "Thomas Wolfe's great heart and wide sympathies took in all mankind."[38] Why, he had deeply loved Asheville in *Look Homeward, Angel*, a book that had now become "the record of a sensitive soul exploring the hard facts of life for the first time." In such a work any other town would have looked just as bad, not because the town

[37] *Ibid.*, July 5, 1939.
[38] *Ibid.*, February 22, 1939.

was bad, but because "it is of necessity that in some human parade ground each of us must find out for himself the nature of the universe"—whatever that means.

In June the Bon Marche store had a Wolfe display not long before the publication of *The Web and the Rock.* With this book there was one familiar note: the Asheville bookstores had "an unprecedented number of advance orders."[39] But this time sensation was caused by fame and favorable publicity. When the reporter glanced at the past, there was none of the old bitterness. *Look Homeward, Angel,* he ventured, had been "a sensation here because of its amazing realism." Shades of the dead and buried gossips! The sword had been hung up to rust. In the same article there were innocuous notes on the source of "Child by Tiger" and on the change from Altamont to Libya Hill.[40] *The Web and the Rock* was reviewed three days later by a writer designated "O.C.D." This critic in the new order found the book filled with "wonderful writing" and displaying "power and passion, with vitality and drive." Then he ventured a timid statement that the writers of the old days would have laughed off the press. He thought the "crushing realism" matched that of the previous novels, especially in "his description of the tenement district and its population in his home town."[41] But this was a mild complaint, and the *Citizen* in October divided those in Asheville who read Wolfe's works into two categories: "worshippers and casual readers."[42]

After the turbulent reception of *Look Homeward, Angel* and the interest given to *The Web and the Rock,* the attention that *You Can't Go Home Again* attracted when it came out in

[39] *Ibid.,* June 22, 1939.
[40] *Ibid.*
[41] *Ibid.,* June 25, 1939.
[42] *Ibid.,* October 8, 1939.

1940 was most anticlimactic. The *Citizen* of September 22 published a short review that, amazingly, paid as much attention to form as it did to source. *You Can't Go Home Again,* in the reviewer's opinion, is "no story, but rather is a rambling, narrative account of the events in the life of one individual." This reception provoked one reader to write a letter to the editor objecting because of the little amount of praise given to Wolfe's last complete work.[43]

In 1941 came *The Hills Beyond,* the last of the posthumous books. In the *Citizen's* review, by Walter S. Adams, there is no reference to the old problem of autobiography beyond the suggestion that Ashevillians puzzled about why Wolfe wrote *Look Homeward, Angel* might find the answer in *The Hills Beyond.* The news that "the tremendous eloquence of this famous son of Asheville is stilled"[44] was a message of sorrow, although ten years before, the same message would have caused many to chortle with glee.

The summation of the town's attitude from 1941 to the present is an account of the steady growth of the fame of a native genius; and literally thousands of articles published on Wolfe, his family, his teachers, his schools, his friends, indeed, on all that he encountered reveal the frantic journalistic and municipal efforts to sweep up the last tidbits of genius and fame. The Asheville public library, which long before had banned his books, had an exhibit of Wolfe's works and some of his belongings and pictures in 1941, about the time of the publication of *The Hills Beyond.* Now the library is often filled with native and out-of-town Wolfe fans reading newspaper articles about Wolfe and looking at clippings, photographs, books, and

[43] *Ibid.,* September 29, 1940.
[44] *Ibid.,* November 9, 1941.

scrapbooks. In 1941, there was a long article by Don Bishop in the *Citizen* about Wolfe's college prize essay at the University of North Carolina,[45] and the *Times* became excited because an elementary textbook had misspelled his name and made an error in the date of his death.[46]

There have been long accounts in the papers of the death of Mrs. Wolfe; stories about "The '49 Thomas Wolfe Boom," also known as "Thomas Wolfe Week in Asheville"; an account of placing flowers on his grave; editorials on the family's influence on the son; reprinted articles and editorials from out-of-town newspapers; stories of library exhibitions on his birthday; a review of the *Portable Thomas Wolfe* ("In the pitchman's lingo, Wolfe is today a hot item"); an editorial on "Tom Wolfe's Half-Century"; accounts of what old friends knew and thought about him; stories of the deaths of characters in the books (at least once headlined by the fictitious rather than the real name[47]); accounts of the deaths of Wolfe's elementary-school teachers; an article describing the Old Kentucky Home as a blight on the landscape and saying it should be torn down because Wolfe and other people hated it; a restrained announcement of the discovery of the real angel in 1949; stories about John Skally Terry, Maxwell Perkins, Edward C. Aswell; radio programs; and a projected motion picture based on *Look Homeward, Angel.* There have been and still are Wolfe dinners, speeches, memorials, collections, tributes, foundations, drives, and meets.

In 1948, the family offered the Old Kentucky Home for sale in a want ad; they preferred that it become a shrine, "but will

45 *Ibid.*, April 20, 1941.
46 *Asheville Times*, February 28, 1941.
47 *Ibid.*, August 14, 1947.

consider a sale for other purposes."[48] It became a shrine, and all the paraphernalia of the novels sit today as they were seen long years ago by Thomas Wolfe and Eugene Gant. The town fairly glows with pride. The newspaper apologizes for the Tarheels who were insulted by his books,[49] and the town glories in its recognition of his artistry before his death. "From that spirit world to which he has gone," the *Citizen* poeticized in 1952, "Thomas Wolfe must look back with happy surprise and feel a warm pleasure in the proud boast that Asheville and North Carolina now makes [*sic*] of their famous novelist."[50]

In 1953, a reader of the *Asheville Citizen-Times,* impressed with the flowing tributes to the most famous native son, predicted "The Triple-Decker Wolfeburger," "Ye Olds [*sic*] Wolfe Tea Room," the "Thomas Wolfe Honest Auto Traders," and "The Look Homeward, Angel Motel."[51]

The going home of genius, even after death, is a complicated process. One must welcome the prodigal.

48 *Ibid.*, July 7, 1948.
49 *Asheville Citizen,* October 5, 1952.
50 *Ibid.*
51 *Ibid.*, April 26, 1953.

9. The Sum of All the Moments

A STUDY of how Asheville became Altamont and Libya Hill, of how the Wolfes became Gants and Joyners, of how Tom became Eugene and George is most difficult and complicated; but this problem alone is only a small part of a study of Wolfe and Asheville. The creative genius of Tom Wolfe presented the town in fiction, which in turn changed the town in reality when it was read by the citizens, whose violent emotions then caused changes in Tom Wolfe. There was a chain reaction, and always an effect became a cause of some new phenomenon. But time, Wolfe said, "puts halters to debate." The bitterness and antagonism changed to adulation, and he did not like that either.

Over many years there were charges and great bitterness, and Wolfe felt compelled to reply and debate. Yet he did protest too much. What would have happened, one may speculate, if he had omitted the single clause of dispute from the address "To the Reader" at the beginning of *Look Homeward, Angel*: "He would insist that this book is a fiction, and that he meditated no man's portrait here."

Usually he identified himself as a writer, not as a novelist. Why not "essayist," "historian"? The problem is not so easy.

; of examples might show how the works are a strange f reality and the imagination. Even those formalists t that the books are not novels would be compelled ... that they are not history or essays either. Wolfe never wished to be a historian. Scholars, he thought, are pedants who devote themselves slavishly to fact, and for him the fact was apparently necessary but never unalterable, never true for its own sake. It was a subjective truth, a combination of external reality and internal lyrical thought.

The charge of autobiography infuriated Wolfe because it made him a noncreative writer, an essayist, a historian of self. Asheville's attitude gave additional evidence that he dealt in facts rather than in art. He was, then, affronted artistically as well as personally. That he was himself ready to explode before Asheville lighted the fuse is shown by some of the points of view in *Look Homeward, Angel,* as well as by his statements before the book was published. One major theme of this first novel, as of all those that came later, was the aspiration of a young Southerner to be a writer despite a hostile environment. From the time when Wolfe began writing one-act plays for the Carolina Playmakers until he wrote his last book, he struggled, in his own mind at least, against family, environment, lovers, and friends; he strove to be sincere and to develop his own art. Thus, he saw the controversy over *Look Homeward, Angel* merely as a decisive battle in a long campaign. That his home town should not recognize and praise his creativeness was nearly unbearable.

He wanted his family and the people of Asheville to admire Thomas Wolfe as a creator of imaginary people. When they recognized his supposedly fictitious characters, he was more hurt because he knew the truth of their charges. Perhaps he saw in their reactions a self-criticism that was indeed so painful that he constantly thrust it into his subconscious mind and refused to let himself think about the problem. He could find enough of the creative in his works to support his convictions that they were much more than journalistic accounts of the sources. He had given the material what Randall Stewart has called a "framed created meaning," and in his own mind he usually tried to forget his use of the innate meaning of the fact or the material.

Wolfe's error in creation was the failure to associate the type and the individual. When, for example, he created a character and fitted his personality into the pattern and framework of one of his books, he did so because in life he had known such a real person. Seldom, indeed, did he weave a figure mainly from the fabric of his imagination and use threads from the lives of many people. Frequently, and especially in the later books, he created a character on the basis of one prototype but selected additional traits from other people. His memory for the specific enabled him to portray characters that are supremely vivid, yet the same quality also perhaps caused his failure to select details he wanted from many sources. To generalize and combine, he seems to have thought, would be to lose particularity. Thus, Uncle Bascom is H. A. Westall, not a combination of dozens of personalities whom Wolfe had known. And almost every portrait that flowed from his pen was created exactly as Uncle Bascom was.

He recalled not only sensations that he had experienced but also the specific emotional reactions that had come as a result of the sensations. This ability is probably responsible for Wolfe's power in making his readers poignantly feel the transience of life. "But we are the sum of all the moments of our lives—" he told his readers before he began his narrative in *Look Homeward, Angel,* "all that is ours is in them: we cannot escape or conceal it. If the writer has used the clay of life to make his book, he has only used what all men must, what none can keep from using." Wolfe persisted, however, in seeing each figure or moment of action exactly as it was. He was so much attracted by life as it actually existed, he saw so much in each unit of it, that he simply did not wish to see anything altered. Seldom did he add a detail or even change a sequence. Life had for him the innate integrity that other writers find only after they have made great alterations. Often he seems to have been motivated by the belief that life itself is the greatest work of art and that even selection violates the innate form of the raw material.

Those who sit in judgment on this belief must keep in mind the truth that within the covers of any book there is no artistic distinction between fiction presented with verisimilitude and fact presented with artistry. The use of autobiography is not in itself an artistic weakness. Instead, those who demand that fiction be entirely an invented story may have a false and naïve standard, which, if imposed, would result in the damnation of nearly all fiction, including the works of Fitzgerald, Lewis, Maugham, Twain, Joyce, and Faulkner. Even an artist like Maugham has written that *Of Human Bondage* "is not an autobiography, but an autobiographical novel; fact and fiction are inextricably mingled; the emotions are my own, but not all the incidents are related as they happened and some of them are transferred to my hero not from my own life but from that of persons with whom I was intimate." The same statement is true of *Look Homeward, Angel,* and it is even more accurate for all Wolfe's other works. There is a degree of difference in the amount of transference and mingling. But the greatest contrast between Wolfe and other authors lies perhaps in the sensationalism that fatally shadowed the hulking frame of Tom Wolfe.

"For the imagination never operates in a vacuum," John Livingston Lowes wrote at the end of *The Road to Xanadu.* "Its stuff is always fact of some order, somehow experienced; its product is that fact transmuted." If Wolfe's experience, environment, and temperament were such as to demand less transmutation, the result is not necessarily that the work of art is inferior. Even the great masters, Lowes admitted, sometimes allow facts to "swamp imagination, and [to] remain unassimilated and untransformed."

Surviving records, letters, and accounts of talks by Wolfe's family and friends make it possible in hundreds of instances to see reality before it was transformed into art. Yet even here the critic's analytical mind is limited and the working of genius is inexplicable and shrouded in mystery. Exactly how he created, even Wolfe himself did not know. Hundreds of youths in hundreds of towns have most of the ingredients, but there is no pattern that shows others how to create. One cannot follow Wolfe's methods and set out to record a town.

Wolfe was at his best when he did record his home town and the South, that "Dark Helen in Eugene's blood." "His feeling for the South," he wrote, "was not so much historic as it was of the core and desire of dark romanticism—that unlimited and inexplicable drunkenness, the magnetism of some men's blood that takes them into the heart of the heat, and beyond that, into the polar and emerald cold of the South. . . ." Early in his writing career George Webber tried "to set down the shape and feel of that one year in childhood." This project grew until he wished "to present the picture, not merely of his youth, but of the whole town from which he came, and all the people in it just as he had known them." Finally, he hoped, he would encompass a larger world and the strands of his work "would take on the denseness and complexity of the whole web of life and of America." In this objective, if not in craftsmanship, he was successful. Cosmopolitan and provincial Asheville proved to be a microcosm that provided subject matter and a standard of reference throughout Wolfe's career. Truly, the land of his origins was the "Dark Helen" of his blood.

Index

The names of characters and places in Wolfe's fiction are followed by an asterisk.